LEED v4
AP O+M
MOCK EXAM

Questions, Answers, and Explanations: A Must-Have for the LEED AP O+M Exam, Green Building LEED Certification, and Sustainability

Gang Chen
ArchiteG®, Inc.
Irvine, California

LEED v4 AP O+M MOCK EXAM: Questions, Answers, and Explanations: A Must-Have for the LEED AP O&M Exam, Green Building LEED Certification, and Sustainability

Copyright © 2017   Gang Chen
Edition 1.0

Cover Photo © 2017   Gang Chen. All rights reserved.

Copy Editor: Penny L Kortje

All Rights Reserved.
No part of this book may be transmitted or reproduced by any means or in any form, including electronic, graphic, or mechanical, without the express written consent of the publisher or author, except in the case of brief quotations in a review.

ArchiteG®, Inc.
http://www.ArchiteG.com
http://www.GreenExamEducation.com

ISBN: 978-1-61265-030-2
PRINTED IN THE UNITED STATES OF AMERICA

What others are saying about LEED AP O+M Mock Exam ...

"These are TOUGH sample tests. You need this book.!
"I used this book as a review in the day or two before my exam. The questions in this book could very well be found on the exam, but most actual exam questions will not be as complex as they are made here. Most of these questions on these mock exams have a twist or trick and many can only be answered if you know the materials backwards and forward. This makes for GREAT exam preparation because it makes you acutely aware of the types of tricks and the level of detail you MIGHT see on the exam..."
— G. Patton

"I highly recommend this book!
"The book was extremely helpful for me passing the exam. The questions really challenged me to dig deeper into the details of each category. I felt this was one of several tools to help me be prepared for the exam. I highly recommend this book."
— Edwin F Sierra

"Such a great tool!
"I passed the exam at the first attempt. These mock exams helped me to learn how to tackle the problems and which areas I should focus on! I worked with another book of the author also. It took 2-3 weeks for my preparation."
— Chai

Dedication

To my parents, Zhuixian and Yugen,
my wife Xiaojie, and my daughters
Alice, Angela, Amy, and Athena.

Disclaimer

This book provides general information about the LEED AP O+M Exam and green building LEED Certification. It is sold with the understanding that the publisher and author are not providing legal, accounting, or other professional services. If legal, accounting, and other professional services are required, seek the services of a competent professional firm.

It is not the purpose of this book to reprint the content of all other available texts on the subject. You are urged to read other available texts and tailor them to fit your needs.

Great effort has been made to make this book as complete and accurate as possible; however, nobody is perfect, and there may be typographical or other mistakes. You should use this book as a general guide and not as the ultimate source on this subject.

This book is intended to provide general, entertaining, informative, educational, and enlightening content. Neither the publisher nor the author shall be liable to anyone or any entity for any loss or damages, or alleged loss and damages, caused directly or indirectly by the content of this book.

ArchiteG®, Green Associate Exam Guide®, GA Study®, and GreenExamEducation® are registered trademarks owned by Gang Chen.

ARE®, Architect Registration Examination® are registered trademarks owned by NCARB.

USGBC® and LEED® are trademarks of the US Green Building Council. The US Green Building Council is not affiliated with the publication of this book.

TABLE OF CONTENTS

Preface **13**

LEED Exam Guides series by ArchiteG, Inc **19**

**Strategies for Preparing for
LEED AP O+M Exam** **23**

**Chapter One   LEED AP O+M Mock Exam
(Including Both Part One and Part Two)** **27**
    I.   Important Note: Read this before you work on AP BD+C Mock Exam 28
    II.   LEED AP O+M Mock Exam 29

**Chapter Two   LEED AP O+M Mock Exam Answers
and Explanations (Including Both Part One and Part Two)** **85**
    I.   Answers and Explanations for the LEED AP O+M Mock Exam Part One 85
    II.   Answers and Explanations for the LEED AP O+M Mock Exam Part Two 109
    III. How was the LEED AP O+M Mock Exam created? 147
    IV. Where can I find the latest and official sample questions for the LEED AP O+M Exam? .147
    V.   Latest trend for LEED Exams 148
    VI. LEED AP O+M Exam registration............ 150

Chapter Three Frequently Asked Questions (FAQ) and Other Useful Resources **153**

- I. I found the reference guide way too tedious. Can I only read your book and just refer to the USGBC reference guide (if one is available for the exam I am taking) when needed?... 153
- II. Is one week really enough for me to prepare for the exam while I am working? 153
- III. Would you say that if I buy your LEED exam guide series books, I could pass the exam using no other study materials? The books sold on the USGBC website run in the hundreds of dollars, so I would be quite happy if I could buy your book and just use that. 154
- IV. I am preparing for the LEED exam. Do I need to read the 2" thick reference guide? 156
- V. For LEED v4, will the total number of points be more than 110 in total if a project gets all of the extra credits and all of the standard credits? 156
- VI. For the exam, do I need to know the project phase in which a specific prerequisite/credit takes place? (i.e., pre-design, schematic design, etc.) 157
- VII. Are you writing new versions of books for the new LEED exams? What new books are you writing?.. 158
- VIII. Important documents that you need to download for free, become familiar with and memorize 158
- IX. Important documents that you need to download for free, and become familiar with 159
- X. Do I need to take many practice questions to prepare for a LEED exam?........................ 161

Appendixes **165**
   I.   Default occupancy factors 165
   II.   Official reference materials listed by
          the GBCI 166
   III.   Important resources and further study
          materials you can download for free 169
   IV.   Annotated bibliography 171
   V.   Valuable web sites and links 172
   VI.   Important Items Covered by the Second
          Edition of *Green Building and LEED Core*
          Concepts Guide 174

Back Page Promotion **181**
   I.   *ARE Mock Exam series*
          (GreenExamEducation.com) 182
   II.   LEED Exam Guides series 185
   III.   Building Construction (ArchiteG.com) 194
   IV.   Planting Design Illustrated 196

Index **199**

Preface

The USGBC released LEED v4 in GreenBuild International Conference and Expo in November 2013. The GBCI started to include the new LEED v4 content for all LEED exams in June 2014. We have incorporated the new LEED v4 content in this book.

Starting on December 1, 2011, GBCI began to draw LEED AP O+M Exam questions from the second edition of *Green Building and LEED Core Concepts Guide*. We have incorporated this latest information in our books. See Appendix 5 for Important Items Covered by the Second Edition of *Green Building and LEED Core Concepts Guide*.

There are two main purposes for this book: to help you pass the LEED AP O+M (Operation + Maintenance) Exam and to assist you with understanding the process of getting a building LEED certified.

The LEED AP O+M Exam has two parts (or sections):

Part One is EXACTLY the same as the LEED Green Associate Exam. It has 100 multiple choice questions and must be finished within two hours (The total exam time for BOTH parts of the exam is four hours). In this book, "LEED AP O+M Exam Part One," "LEED AP O+M Exam Section One," and "LEED Green Associate Exam" are used interchangeably since they are EXACTLY the same.

Part Two is the LEED AP O+M specialty exam. It focuses on information and knowledge related directly to green building operation + maintenance (O+M). It also contains 100 multiple choice questions and must be finished within two hours.

You can take Part One first, pass it, and gain a title of LEED Green Associate and then take Part Two in a different setting, or you can take both sections (Part One and Part Two) of the LEED AP O+M Exam back-to-back in the same sitting. When a test taker fails one of the two parts, he can retake only the failed section of the exam at a later date.

The raw exam score is converted to a scaled score ranging from 125 to 200. The passing score is 170 or higher. You need to answer <u>about</u> 60 questions correctly for each section to pass. There is an optional 10-minute tutorial for computer testing before the exam and an optional 10-minute exit survey.

The LEED Green Associate Exam is the most important LEED exam for two reasons:

1. You have to pass it in order to get the title of LEED Green Associate.

2. It is also the required <u>Part One</u> (2 hours) of <u>ALL</u> LEED AP+ exams. You have to pass it plus Part Two (2 hours) of the specific LEED AP+ exam of your choice to get any LEED AP+ title unless you have passed the old LEED AP exam before June 30, 2009.

There are a few ways to prepare for the LEED AP

O+M Exam:

1. You can take USGBC courses or workshops. You should take USGBC classes at both the 100 (Awareness) and 200 (LEED Core Concepts and Strategies) level to successfully prepare for Part One of the exam. USGBC classes at 300 level (Green Building Design & Construction: The LEED Implementation Process) can be taken to prepare for Part Two of the exam. A one-day course normally costs $445 (as of publication) with an early registration discount, otherwise it is $495. You will also have to wait until the USGBC workshops or courses are offered in a city near you.

OR
2. Take USGBC online courses. Refer to the USGBC or GBCI websites for information. The USGBC online courses are less personal and still expensive.

OR
3. Read related books. Unfortunately, there are few official USGBC books on the LEED AP O+M Exam. *LEED v4 O+M Mock Exam* is one of the first books covering this subject and will fill in this blank to assist you with passing the exam.

To stay at the forefront of the LEED and green building movement and make my books more valuable to their readers, I sign up for USGBC courses and workshops myself. I review the USGBC and GBCI websites and many other sources to get as much information as possible on LEED. *LEED v4 O+M Mock Exam & the upcoming LEED v4 O+M Exam Guide* are a result of this very comprehensive research. I have done the hard work so that you can save time preparing for the exam by reading this book.

Strategy 101 for the LEED AP O+M Exam is that you must recognize that you have only a limited amount of time to prepare for the exam. So, you must concentrate your time and effort on the most important content of the LEED AP O+M Exam.

LEED v4 O+M Mock Exam provides you with a complete set of mock exams, including questions, answers, and explanations.

Most people already have some knowledge of LEED. I suggest that you use a highlighter when you read this book; you can highlight the content that you are not familiar with when you read the book for the first time. Try covering the answer and then read the question. If you come up with the correct answer before you read the book, you do not need to highlight the question and answer. If you cannot come up with the correct answer before you read the book, then highlight that question. This way, when you do your review later and read the book for the second time, you can focus on the portions that you are not familiar with and save yourself a lot of time. You can repeat this process with different colored highlighters until you are very familiar with the content of this book. Then, you will be ready to take the LEED AP O+M Exam.

The key to passing the LEED AP O+M Exam, or any other exam, is to know the scope of the exam, and not to read too many books. Select one or two really good books and focus on them. Actually <u>understand</u> the content and memorize it. For your convenience, I have underlined the fundamental information that I think is very important. You definitely need to memorize all the information that I have underlined. You should try to understand the content first, and then memorize the content of the book by reading it multiple times. This is a much better way than "mechanical" memory without understanding.

There is a part of the LEED AP O+M Exam that you can control by reading study materials: the section regarding the number of points and credit process for the LEED building rating system. Become very familiar with every major credit category and try to answer all questions related to this part correctly.

There is also a part of the exam that you may not be able to control. You may not have done actual LEED building certification, so there will be some questions that may require you to guess. This is the hardest part of the exam, but these questions should be only a small percentage of the test if you are well prepared. Eliminate the obvious wrong answers and then attempt an educated guess. There is no penalty for guessing. If you have no idea what the correct answer is and cannot eliminate any obvious wrong answer, then do not waste too much time on the question, just pick a guess answer. The key is, try to use the same guess answer for all of the questions that you are completely unsure of. For example, if you choose "a" as the guess answer, then be consistent and use "a" as the guess answer for all the questions that are completely unsure of. That way, you likely have a better chance of guessing more correct answers.

This is not an easy exam, but you should be able to pass it if you prepare well. If you set your goal for a high score and study hard, you will have a better chance of passing. If you set your goal for the minimum passing score of 170, you will probably end up scoring 169 and fail, and you will have to retake the exam again. That will be the last thing you want. Give yourself plenty of time and do not wait until the last minute to begin preparing for the exam. I have met people who have spent 40 hours preparing and passed the exam, but I suggest that you give yourself at least two to three weeks of preparation time. On the night before the exam, look through the questions on the mock exam that you did not answer correctly and remember what the correct answers are. Read this book carefully, prepare well, relax and put yourself in the best physical, mental and psychological state on the day of the exam, and you will pass.

LEED Exam Guides series by ArchiteG, Inc.

Time and effort is the most valuable asset of a candidate. How to cherish and effectively use your limited time and effort is the key of passing any exam. That is why we publish the LEED Exam Guides series to help you to study and pass the LEED exams in the shortest time possible. We have done the hard work so that you can save time and money. We do not want to make you work harder than you have to.

Do not force yourself to memorize a lot of numbers. Read through the numbers a few times, and you should have a very good impression of them.

You need to make the judgment call: If you miss a few numbers, you can still pass the exam, but if you spend too much time drilling these numbers, you may miss out on the big pictures and fail the exam.

There are only a small number of official GBCI sample questions without explanations in the candidate handbook. The USGBC has been separated from GBCI and should have no clue of how GBCI constructs the LEED exam questions. Otherwise, the LEED exams will NOT be legally defensible. The existing practice questions or exams by others are either way too easy or way over-killed. They do NOT match the real LEED exams at all.

We have done very comprehensive research on the official GBCI guides, many related websites, reference materials, and other available LEED exam prep materials. We match our mock exams questions as close as possible to the GBCI samples and the real LEED exams. Some other readers had failed an LEED exam two or three times before, and they eventually passed the exam with our help.

Some authors rewrite the same information in a generic format for LEED Green Associate Exam, but I prefer to follow the LEED rating systems format that used by the USGBC for both exams and the related exam reference guides and not reinvent the wheel.

This will save you time because you know exactly what you have already studied after you have prepared for LEED Green Associate Exam, which is the same as part I of the LEED AP O+M exam. You just need to spend maybe 30% more time (instead of double) to study for part II of the LEED AP O+M exam (specialty exam).

After studying my books, you will become very familiar the LEED rating systems and you will be able to quickly locate the information in the USGBC reference guide when you work on the actual LEED projects. In fact, many of my readers simply use my book 90% of the time, and just use the USGBC reference guide to look up some very detailed information.

Other books on LEED Exams will become almost useless instantly once you pass the exam because they are NOT designed as a reference book, while my book becomes even more valuable AFTER the exam.

All our guide books include study guide, a set of sample questions matching the real LEED exams, including number of questions, format, type of questions, etc. We also include detailed answers and explanations to our questions.

There is some extra information on LEED overviews and exam-taking tips in Chapter One. This is based on GBCI AND other valuable sources. This is a bonus feature we included in each book because we want our readers to be able to buy our LEED mock exam books together or individually. We want you to find all necessary LEED exam information and resources at one place and through our books.

All our books are available at
http://www.GreenExamEducation.com

Strategies for Preparing for LEED AP O+M Exam

There are several strategies for preparing for LEED AP O+M Exam:

1. Bare bone strategy:
This strategy is bold, risky, but effective, low cost, and takes the least amount of time. You can spend about two weeks to prepare and pass the exam:

a. Download and read the latest candidate handbook for LEED AP O+M Exam
b. Study the FREE PDF files listed at the end of the latest candidate handbook for LEED AP O+M Exam (About 20% to 30% of the test content will come from these materials).
c. Study my books, *LEED v4 O+M Mock Exam* and the upcoming *LEED v4 O+M Exam Guide* (Covers the fundamental and most important information of the remaining 70% to 80% of test content will come from these materials).
d. Do NOT buy or read the USGBC reference guide AT ALL

Pros:
a. Save time and money and still have a good chance of passing. In fact, a number of my readers did pass the exam using this approach.
b. You can prepare and pass the exam in about **two weeks**.

Cons:
a. Your score may not be as high as you want since you COMPLETELY skip the USGBC reference guide (probably range from 170 to 180).
b. You may feel nervous during the real exam. You may swear that you fail in the exam, and end up passing. You may have no clue why you pass but I know why you pass the exam though: my books cover the fundamental and most important information of the exam and set up a solid foundation for your LEED knowledge.

2. Middle of the road strategy:
This strategy is exactly the same as **bare bone strategy**, except that you do the following extra things:

a. Buy or read portion of the USGBC reference guide to supplement my two books:
Only refer to or read the USGBC reference guide for items you have questions, or for detailed information not covered by my books such as the "Behind the Intent" and "Step-by-Step Guidance" Sections and Calculations. I skip these sections in my book because it takes too much time for you to read the information, and I think you should be able to handle most of the tasks covered in these sections if you MASTER the other sections.
b. Do a few extra sets of mock exams.

Pros:
a. Save time and money and still have an excellent chance of passing. In fact, many readers did pass the exam using this approach.
b. You can prepare and pass the exam in about **two to four weeks**.

Cons:
a. Your score may not be as high as you want (probably range from 170 to 185).
b. You may still feel nervous during the real exam.

3. Comprehensive strategy:
This strategy is exactly the same as **bare bone strategy**, except that you do the following extra things:

a. Buy or read the USGBC reference guide from cover to cover several times.
b. Write your own notes or create your own spread sheets based on the USGBC reference guide.
c. Do every set of mock exams that you can find.

Pros:
a. You have an excellent chance of passing if you can REALLY read the reference guide. In fact, several readers did pass the exam using this approach.

Cons:
a. Your score may be either very high or very low (probably either range from 180 to 200, OR fail).
b. You need to spend two months or more to prepare and pass the exam.
c. You drag the exam prep process too long, and become tired of reading the USGBC reference guide, OR you can NOT find enough time to read the reference guide, and you end up failing the exam.

If you can pass the specialty exam, you should be able to pass the LEED Green Associate Exam. Make sure you download the PDF files listed in the candidate's handbook and peruse them.

All our books are available at **GreenExamEducation**.com

Check out FREE tips and info for all LEED Exams and ARE Exams at **GeeForum.com**, you can post jpeg files of your vignettes or your questions for other users' review and responses.

Chapter One
LEED AP O+M Exam Mock Exam (Including Both Part One and Part Two)

Use the questions from the mock exam to prepare for the real exam. They will give you an idea of what the GBCI is looking for on the LEED AP O+M Exam, and how the questions will be asked. If you can answer 80% of the sample questions correctly, you are ready to take the real exam. The 80% passing score is based on feedback from previous readers. You should read the free study materials listed in my book, at least three times before you attempt the mock exam. Similar to the real exam, a question might ask you to pick one, two, or three correct answers out of four, or four correct answers out of five (some LEED exam questions have five choices). Generally speaking, if you do not know any of the correct answers, then you will probably get the overall answer wrong. You need to know the LEED system very well in order to answer correctly.

I have intentionally included some questions that you may not know the answers to. This is to help you practice making an educated guess.

I. Important Note: Read this before you work on LEED O+M Mock Exam

1. How much time should you spend on preparing for the LEED exam?

Answer: Some people spend too much time preparing for the LEED exam, and by the time they take the real test, they may have forgotten a lot of the information already.

Timing is VERY critical. If you pass the practice test with a score of 190 three months before the real test, by the time you take the test, you may have forgotten the information and score much lower.

One way to overcome this is NOT to take too much time to prepare for the LEED exam, and save at least one set of mock exam to use in the last week before the exam. You should NOT read any questions on this reserved mock exam until one or two weeks before the exam. This way, you can alert and energize yourself one more time right before the real exam, and work on your weaknesses. You can save the LEED AP O+M Mock Exam for this purpose.

There is one reader who passed the LEED Green Associate Exam or Part I of LEED AP O+M Exam by studying my other book, *LEED Green Associate Exam Guide,* for 10 hours in total.

For an average reader, I recommend not less than 2 weeks, but not MORE than 2 months of prep time. If you read my other book, *LEED BD&C Exam Guide*, you'll understand why too much prep time may hurt your chance of passing the exam.

II. LEED AP O+M Mock Exam

Part One:

1. With regard to the credit, Optimize Energy Performance, who has the most influence in decision-making?
   a. MEP Engineer
   b. Architect
   c. Contractor
   d. Health Department Plan Checker

2. A project team should include the following as part of process energy: (Choose 3)
   a. Lighting that is part of the medical equipment
   b. Lighting included as part of the lighting power allowance
   c. Energy for water pumps
   d. HVAC
   e. Energy for elevators and escalators

3. A project team should include the following as part of regulated (non-process) energy: (Choose 3)
   a. Lighting for interiors
   b. Refrigeration and kitchen cooking
   c. Space heating
   d. Service water heating
   e. Energy for computers, office, and general miscellaneous equipment

4. With regard to LEED v4, which of the following LEED rating systems has fewer points for the WE category? (Choose 2)

a. LEED BDC NC
b. LEED BDC CS
c. LEED BDC Schools
d. LEED IDC CI
e. LEED OM EB

5. Which of the following are not considered laws?
   a. USGBC LEED reference guides
   b. Building codes
   c. ADA
   d. Municipal codes
   e. EPA Codes of Federal Regulations

6. Which of the following buildings cannot obtain LEED certification? (Choose 2)
   a. A new building that uses CFC
   b. A new building that does not use CFC
   c. A remodel project with a plan to phase out CFCs in 15 years
   d. A building that uses natural refrigerants
   e. A building that uses dry ice

7. Which of the following can reduce stormwater runoff and alleviate the urban heat island effect? (Choose 3)
   a. Increasing the site coverage ratio
   b. Increasing Floor Area Ratio (FAR)
   c. Using a vegetated roof
   d. Using porous pavement with high albedo
   e. Building a retention pond on the site

8. Recycled materials will contribute to which of the following?
   a. Traffic alleviation and smog reduction
   b. Protection of virgin materials
   c. Energy savings

d. MEP cost savings
9. Which of the following is not graywater?
   a. Water from kitchen sinks
   b. Water from toilet
   c. Harvest rainwater
   d. Water from outdoor area drains
   e. None of above
   f. All of above

10. Which of the following is not blackwater? (Choose 2)
    a. Water from kitchen sinks
    b. Water from toilets
    c. Harvest rainwater
    d. Water from floor drains
    e. Rainwater that has come into contact with animal waste

11. Which of the following is not true? (Choose 2)
    a. Water from kitchen sinks can be reused for landscape irrigation or flushing toilets.
    b. Water from kitchen sinks cannot be reused for landscape irrigation or flushing toilets.
    c. Reclaimed water requires special piping with a different color.
    d. Reclaimed water cannot reduce potable water use.

12. Which of the following sets the baseline for water use? (Choose 2)
    a. Energy Policy Act (EPAct) of 1992
    b. Uniform Plumbing Code (UPC)
    c. WaterSense standards
    d. International Plumbing Code (IPC)

13. Which of the following sets the minimum standard of water use reduction?
    a. Energy Policy Act (EPAct) of 1992
    b. Uniform Plumbing Codes (UPC)
    c. WaterSense standards
    d. International Plumbing Code (IPC)

14. The State of California is building a visitor center on a 200,000 sf park. How big does the visitor center need to be, in order to meet the MPRs for LEED?
    a. 1,000 sf
    b. 2,000 sf
    c. 3,000 sf
    d. 4,000 sf
    e. There is not enough information to determine the minimum sf of the visitor center.

15. What is the maximum number of Regional Priority points a project can achieve?
    a. 3
    b. 4
    c. 5
    d. 6

16. The LEED O&M rating system is different from other LEED rating systems in which of the following ways:
    a. The LEED O&M rating system can be applied to any building type.
    b. The LEED O&M rating system emphasizes measuring and verification.
    c. The LEED O&M rating system emphasizes life cycle costing.
    d. The LEED O&M rating system deals with

buildings after construction is completed.
17. Which program is used to qualify off-site green power for LEED?
   a. Green-e
   b. Center for Resource Solution
   c. Green Label
   d. Green Certified

18. Which of the following is the best to measure a material's ability to reflect sunshine?
   a. Albedo
   b. SRI
   c. Color
   d. Hue

19. Which of the following will not reduce materials sent to landfill? (Choose 2)
   a. Recycling
   b. Reusing materials
   c. Using regrounded materials
   d. Reducing materials used
   e. Reworking

20. Which of the following will not reduce materials sent to recycling facilities?
   a. Recycling
   b. Reusing materials
   c. Reducing materials used
   d. Reworking

21. Which of the following is the best statement regarding water savings for LEED credits?
   a. Water savings for LEED credits are per building codes.
   b. Water savings for LEED credits are per green

building codes.
c. Water savings for LEED credits are per federal regulations.
d. Water savings for LEED credits are based on the percentage of water savings achieved by each design case as compared with a baseline building.

22. Which of the following is the best way to alleviate suburban sprawl?
   a. Build more low-rise, high-density housing.
   b. Provide underground parking spaces.
   c. Improve community connectivity.
   d. Provide more pedestrian walkways.

23. A developer has selected an urban site near a shopping center. This will help which of the following?
   a. Community connectivity
   b. Reducing urban runoff
   c. Community relationship
   d. Minimum city code requirements

24. Which of the following is considered open spaces for a LEED project?
   a. Landscape areas
   b. Tennis courts
   c. Sidewalks
   d. Areas under canopy
   e. Atriums with views to the ocean

25. A project seeking LEED certification may incur extra time for the following except:
   a. team member meetings.
   b. a city's plan check.
   c. commissioning.

d. construction administration.

26. When should a project team start to plan a building's LEED certification?
    a. At schematic design
    b. At design development
    c. At pre-design stage
    d. At construction stage

27. For LEED certification, you should include the following as part of the project's area except:
    a. a parking lot.
    b. a landscape area.
    c. an interior space.
    d. a shared parking structure on an adjacent property.

28. A project team is working on a LEED BDC NC project. How much CFC-refrigerant can the team use?
    a. 2%
    b. 5%
    c. 7%
    d. None

29. Green-e is used for which of the following?
    a. On-site green energy
    b. On-site renewable energy
    c. Off-site renewable energy
    d. None of the above

30. Zero Emission Vehicles (ZEV) are defined by the standards set up by: (Choose 2)
    a. California Air Resources Board
    b. Center for Resource Solution
    c. ACEEE

d. SCAQMD

31. You are working on a remodel project seeking LEED certification. What should you do about the existing HVAC units containing CFCs?
   a. Replace CFCs with dry ice.
   b. Replace CFCs with natural refrigerant.
   c. Replace CFCs with halons.
   d. Phase out CFCs in 10 years.

32. Which of the following is graywater?
   a. Water from bathroom sinks and kitchen sinks
   b. Water from bathtubs
   c. Water from toilets
   d. Rainwater collected in cisterns
   e. Stormwater that has not come in contract with toilet waste

33. For a building using a halon-based fire suppression system, which of the following is true? (Choose 2)
   a. Halons cause damage to the ozone layer.
   b. This building cannot seek LEED certification.
   c. This building must meet Fire Department requirements concerning halons.
   d. The halons must have a leakage rate of 10% or less.

34. What is the fundamental reason for global warming?
   a. Too many cars on the street
   b. The use of biofuel
   c. Too many green houses were built in the past century
   d. Too much Carbon dioxide
   e. Too much carbon monoxide

35. SMACNA address which of the following items related to LEED?
    a. Metal work
    b. VOCs
    c. Air quality during construction
    d. ODP
    e. Certified wood

36. For a project's initial research, what are some of the most important local issues? (Choose 3)
    a. Site orientation
    b. Parking regulations
    c. Incentives for sustainable design
    d. ACEEE
    e. TRCs

37. Which of the following statements are not true? (Choose 2)
    a. Bicycle racks will help community connectivity.
    b. High SRI pavement will alleviate the heat island effect.
    c. Green roofs can reduce stormwater runoff and alleviate the heat island effect.
    d. Retention ponds will not reduce stormwater runoff.

38. A construction waste management plan should include which of the following?
    a. The recycling capacity of the neighborhood recycle center
    b. Materials to be used for alternative daily cover (ADC)
    c. If the existing ceiling should be reused

d. The percentage of reused materials

39. A project team is seeking LEED certification for a building. The project can be certified under either the LEED BDC NC or LEED BDC CS rating system. How should the project team determine which LEED system to use? (Choose 2)
    a. Use the system that can gain most points for LEED.
    b. Ask the landlord for advice.
    c. Use the 40/60 rule.
    d. Make an independent decision.
    e. Use the 30/70 rule.

40. A project team is seeking LEED BDC NC certification for a building. Which of the following is true?
    a. The project team cannot seek precertification as a marketing tool for funding and attracting tenants.
    b. The project team can seek precertification as a marketing tool for funding and attracting tenants.
    c. The project must have a signed lease or LOI for at least 70% of the spaces.
    d. The project must be located in a new neighborhood.

41. A project team created a drive-by recycling program for the general public to recycle batteries and used electronics. The project team can gain a point under which of the following categories?
    a. SS
    b. MR
    c. IN
    d. EQ

42. What kinds of energy will generate the most pollution? (Choose 3)
    a. Wind
    b. Biofuel
    c. Gas
    d. Natural gas
    e. Nuclear power

43. Which of the following water saving items can be used for outdoor, indoor, and processed water? (Choose 2)
    a. Water efficient fixtures
    b. Sub-meters
    c. Native plants
    d. Water saving education programs

44. Which of the following analyze the potential savings over a building's life span?
    a. ROI
    b. Life-cycle analysis
    c. Life-cycle cost analysis
    d. Life-cycle saving analysis

45. Which of the following includes standards regarding major factors affecting human comfort?
    a. ASHRAE 55-2010
    b. ASHRAE 62.1-2010
    c. Green Label Plus
    d. Green Building Index

46. If you pass the LEED Green Associate Exam, what can you use on your business card?
    a. The GBCI logo
    b. The LEED GA logo per USGBC guidelines

c. The LEED GA logo per GBCI guidelines
d. The LEED Green Associate logo per GBCI guidelines
e. The LEED GA designation only without any logo

47. A tenant purchased some furniture containing VOCs that was manufactured 450 miles from the job site. Which of the following LEED categories will be affected?
    a. SS
    b. EA
    c. MR
    d. EQ
    e. This project cannot seek LEED certification.

48. Green building through a holistic design approach will result in which of the following?
    a. Longer construction time
    b. Shorter construction time
    c. Extra cost
    d. Synergy
    e. Savings over a building's lifetime

49. A project team is seeking LEED certification for an 8-story building. The building has 8 equal floors, and the total square footage of the building is 168,000 sf. What is the building's footprint?
    a. 168,000 sf
    b. 42,000 sf
    c. 21,000 sf
    d. None of the above

50. For the same project mentioned in Question 49, if the total site area is 1 acre, what is the site coverage for this project?
    a. 48%
    b. 46%
    c. 43%
    d. 38%

51. For the same project mentioned in Question 49, if the total buildable site area is 1 acre, what is the FAR for this project?
    a. 438%
    b. 386%
    c. 338%
    d. 298%

52. A project team is working on a LEED project composed of 6 buildings on a campus. Each building is located on a 1 acre parcel of land. How should the project team determine the boundary of the LEED project?
    a. Each building should have its own LEED project boundary at the edge of the 1 acre land.
    b. The LEED project boundary should be the perimeter of the 6-acre site.
    c. The project team can make its own decision and determine the LEED project boundary.
    d. There is not enough information to determine the LEED project boundary.

53. A LEED project's landscape area includes which of the following?
    a. Green roofs
    b. Naturalistically designed retention ponds
    c. Sidewalks
    d. Vegetated roofs

54. Which of the following only applies to the LEED EQ category?
    a. ASHRAE Advanced Energy Design Guide for Retail Buildings 2010
    b. ASHRAE Standard 55-2010
    c. ASHRAE 62.1-2010
    d. ASHRAE/IESNA Standard 90.1-2010

55. Which of the following is considered a project soft cost?
    a. Carpet
    b. Doors
    c. Permit Fees
    d. Trees and shrubs

56. Where can a LEED Green Associate find the latest errata for LEED reference guides online?
    a. www.gbci.org
    b. www.nrdc.org
    c. www.usgbc.org
    d. www.epa.gov

57. The heat island effect can typically create _____ degrees Fahrenheit of change in temperature?
    a. 1
    b. 5
    c. 10
    d. 20

58. Who rules on CIRs?
    a. The Technical Advisory Group
    b. The LEED Administrator
    c. GBCI
    d. USGBC

59. Which of the following standards specifies minimum ventilation rates for IAQ Performance?
    a. ASHRAE 52.2-2007
    b. ASHRAE 62.1-2010
    c. ASHRAE/IESNA Standard 90.1-2010
    d. ASTM

60. Who of the following publishes GWP and ODP scores?
    a. The World Meteorological Organization
    b. ASTM
    c. USGBC
    d. The Global Climate Control Board

61. Which of the following are the most commonly used energy codes in the United States?
    a. Universal Energy Conservation Codes
    b. IPC by International Code Council
    c. International Energy Conservation Codes
    d. Energy Rating Codes

62. Which of the following is the most effective way to reduce stormwater runoff?
    a. Building a roof with high SRI value
    b. Using pavers with high albedo
    c. Grouping buildings together
    d. Adding trees to a parking lot

63. Which of the following sites is the best for community connectivity?
    a. A site close to the ocean
    b. A site close to a train station
    c. A brownfield site
    d. A site close to a shopping center

64. Choose the non-alternative-fuel vehicle from the following.
    a. A hybrid car
    b. A bus powered by natural gas with at least 20 mpg
    c. A fuel-efficient car powered by gas with at least 40 mpg
    d. An electric car

65. Which of the following is a car share membership program?
    a. Three or more people going to work in the same vehicle
    b. A program in which two or more people share the cost of a parking space
    c. A shuttle service program from a train station to work places
    d. A program for people to rent a vehicle on a daily or hourly basis

66. Which of the following must be certified under only one LEED rating system?
    a. 100% of the LEED project gross floor area
    b. 80% of the LEED project gross floor area
    c. Everything inside the property boundary
    d. 100% of the LEED project gross site area

67. Which of the following is graywater?

a. Stormwater
b. Laundry water
c. Dishwasher water
d. Water in retention ponds

68. Which of the following is used to measure a LEED building's environmental performance?
    a. Life cycle analysis
    b. Cradle-to-cradle analysis
    c. Whole building perspective
    d. Integrated design approach
    e. Overall energy reduction

69. If a LEED project has a CFC phase-out plan, which of the following must occur?
    a. The project can only allow 5% or less of annual CFC leakage.
    b. CFC must be replaced within 15 years.
    c. CFC must be replaced with CO_2.
    d. CFC must be replaced with halons.

70. Which two of the following have the same meaning? (Choose 2)
    a. Albedo
    b. SRI
    c. Refraction
    d. Reflection
    e. Solar Reflectance

71. What are RECs?
    a. The amount of fossil fuels avoided by buying renewable energy and expressed in kilograms
    b. The positive attributes of power generated by renewable sources
    c. The amount of renewable energy purchased

from a third party approved by the Green-e program
d. None of the above

72. The priorities for LEED projects are based on: (Choose 2)
    a. Costs and benefits
    b. Environmental guidelines
    c. Carbon footprint
    d. Project constraints

73. Construction waste reduction strategies include which of the following?
    a. Purchasing materials manufactured locally
    b. Using durable materials
    c. Donating unused materials to charities
    d. Burning the construction waste on site

74. Which of the following is the foundation of the LEED building rating system?
    a. Prerequisites
    b. MPRs
    c. Prerequisites and credits
    d. The triple bottom line

75. A project team is seeking LEED BDC NC certification for a 3-story residential building. Each floor is 600 sf. Which of the following is true?
    a. The project team can seek LEED BDC NC certification because the building is less than 100,000 sf.
    b. The project team can seek LEED BDC NC certification because the building is more than 1,000 sf.
    c. The project team cannot seek LEED BDC

NC certification.
   d. The project team can seek LEED BDC NC certification because it meets LEED's MPRs.

76. Per Montreal Protocol, HCFCs have to be phased out by:
    a. 1995
    b. 2010
    c. 2011
    d. 2030

77. If a building's wastewater overflows, which of the following can come into contact with potable water? (Choose 2)
    a. CO
    b. Toxic metal
    c. Grease
    d. Halons

78. The best way to prevent environmental impact caused by refrigerant leakage is to:
    a. Choose high quality plumbing materials, and perform high quality installation and maintenance.
    b. Use refrigerants without ODP.
    c. Design a building with natural ventilation and use no refrigerants.
    d. None of the above

79. A project team is seeking LEED certification for a single building. What does the LEED project boundary include? (Choose 2)
    a. Only the portion of the site submitted by the project team for LEED certification

b. Overlaps with the edge of the building
c. Overlaps with the edge of the development
d. The entire project scope of work

80. The economic benefits of green buildings include: (Choose 2)
    a. Reduced disturbance of wetland
    b. Lower water bills
    c. Increased use of rapidly renewable materials
    d. Better EQ and less liabilities

81. Which of the following is not a fossil fuel? (Choose 2)
    a. Gas
    b. Natural gas
    c. Biofuel
    d. Solar power

82. Which of the following needs to be implemented for water efficiency?
    a. A baseline of water use
    b. HET
    c. Waterless urinals
    d. Xeriscape

83. Which of the following is the most important feature of durability?
    a. The ability to endure and last for a long time
    b. Low maintenance
    c. Little or no unexpected extra costs
    d. Low maintenance and operation expense over the lifetime of the product

84. A project team is preparing a construction waste management plan. Which of the following should be included? (Choose 2)

a. The removal of refrigerants containing ODP and GWP
b. Recycle areas
c. The removal and disposal of hazardous materials like PCBs
d. The reduction of building size

85. For a LEED project, which of the following should not be used in a fire suppression system? (Choose 2)
    a. Dry ice
    b. Water
    c. HCFCs
    d. CFCs

86. Which of the following can earn points for Innovation? (Choose 2)
    a. Meeting the requirements of all LEED prerequisites and credits
    b. Exceptional performance above and beyond the LEED requirements for an existing credit
    c. Finding a solution responding to the project's regional priorities
    d. Innovative performance in green building categories not covered by an existing LEED credit

87. A project team uses a strategy to earn an Innovation (IN) point for a project in California. Which of the following is true?
    a. The same strategy can be used and guaranteed for an IN point in other projects.
    b. The same strategy can be used for other projects in the same region.

c. The same strategy may or may not earn an IN point in another project.
d. None of the above

88. An office building uses ammonia (NH3) as a refrigerant. Which of the following is true?
   a. NH3 has a higher ODP than HCFC.
   b. NH3 has a lower GWP than HCFC.
   c. NH3 is easier to leak out than HCFC.
   d. CFC is easier to leak out than HCFC.

89. A project team is seeking extra points under the Innovation (IN) credit category. Which of the following is a feasible strategy? (Choose 2)
   a. Set up a display area inside the building to educate the public on this building's LEED performance.
   b. Try to gain more points than the original target level of LEED certification.
   c. Double the performance for a LEED credit.
   d. None of the above
   e. There is not enough information

90. Which of the following can be the most efficient way to save energy?
   a. Proper building orientation and fenestration
   b. High performance HVAC systems
   c. LEED certified equipment
   d. None of the above

91. Which of the following is not true?
   a. A LEED project team has to review the USGBC or GBCI website for previously submitted CIRs before submitting a new one.
   b. A LEED project team has to review the

USGBC reference guide before submitting a CIR.
c. All LEED rating systems can have CIRs except LEED ND.
d. A fee has to be paid for each CIR submitted.

92. ASHRAE standards apply to all of the following except:
    a. SS
    b. WE
    c. EQ
    d. EA

93. Rainwater is:
    a. potable water.
    b. non-potable water.
    c. blackwater.
    d. raw water.
    e. graywater.

94. What are the most important criteria for a LEED building rating system?
    a. Quantifiable performances
    b. Prerequisites
    c. Credits
    d. Third party evaluations
    e. Third party standards

95. Which of the following cannot save water for landscape irrigation? (Choose 2)
    a. Mulches
    b. Perennials
    c. Hardscape
    d. Overhead irrigation
    e. Head to head coverage

96. Which of the following is true with regard to SSC: Heat Island Reduction? (Choose 2)
    a. Temperatures in urban areas can be 22°F (12°C) higher than undeveloped areas and surrounding suburbs.
    b. Urban heat islands contribute to 38.2% of regional warming according to a study of surface warming caused by rapid urbanization in east China.
    c. The solar reflectance index (SRI) is used to measure the solar heat rejection of "non-roof" materials or components that are not considered roofing materials.
    d. Measures to reduce heat islands measures include using a vegetated roof to insulate a building and extend the life of the roof or installing solar panels or shading devices.

97. Which of the following are most appropriate for a vegetated roof?
    a. Native plants
    b. Trees with large canopies
    c. Adaptive plants
    d. Lightweight plants
    e. There is not enough information to answer this question.

98. Which of the following is a prerequisite for purchasing green power? (Choose 3)
    a. The completion of the commissioning plan
    b. Communication with the key stakeholders
    c. Consultation with an electrical engineer
    d. Compilation of energy data
    e. Evaluation of onsite and offsite energy choices

99. Which of the following is a pre-consumer recycled item?
   a. Aluminum storefront created from materials reclaimed from the manufacturing process
   b. Demolition concrete pieces used at another project
   c. Rigid insulation created from materials reclaimed from the manufacturing process of form cornice
   d. Scraps re-used in the carpet manufacturing process

100. A project team is seeking LEED Platinum certification for a school project. When can the project team advise the school board that the LEED Platinum certification has been achieved?
   a. After the project's substantial completion
   b. After the LEED registration is approved
   c. After the design review
   d. After the construction review
   e. After the LEED application is reviewed and approved by GBCI

Part Two:

101. How many categories of certification does LEED O+M include?
    a. 5
    b. 6
    c. 7
    d. 8

102. How many credit categories does LEED O+M include?
    a. 5
    b. 6
    c. 7
    d. 8

103. For a retail building seeking LEED EB:O&M certification, to gain 2 points for WE Credit: Outdoor Water Use Reduction, a project team needs to reduce water use by_____.
    a. 30%
    b. 40%
    c. 50%
    d. 60%

104. For a multifamily building seeking LEED EB:O&M certification, how many points can a project team achieve for having a green cleaning policy in place?
    a. 1
    b. 2
    c. 3
    d. None of above

105. For a Data Center project seeking LEED EB:O&M certification, a project team needs to address all of the following for SS Credit: Site Management except:
    a. Use calcium chloride or sodium chloride deicers, and/or establish reduced treatment areas equal to 50% of applicable paving area.
    b. Prevent erosion and sedimentation, and restore any eroded soils.
    c. Divert from landfills 100% of plant material waste via low-impact means.
    d. Prevent air pollution from construction materials and activities.

106. For a school project seeking LEED EB:O&M certification, regarding MR Credit: Purchasing—Lamps, which of the following statements are not true? (Choose 2)
    a. Implement the lighting purchasing plan that specifies an overall building average of 70 picograms of mercury per lumen-hour or less for all mercury-containing lamps purchased for the building and associated grounds within the project boundary.
    b. Implement the lighting purchasing plan that specifies an overall building average of 20 picograms of mercury per lumen-hour or less for all mercury-containing lamps purchased for the building and associated grounds within the project boundary.
    c. Include lamps for both indoor and outdoor fixtures, as well as both hard-wired and portable fixtures.
    d. Lamps containing no mercury should always be counted.

107. Which of the following are resources for a Level 1 walk-through assessment? (Choose 2)
    a. *2007 ASHRAE Handbook*
    b. *Green-e manual*
    c. *ASHRAE Procedures for Commercial Building Audits*
    d. *Title-24*

108. For MR Credit: Purchasing—Lamps, the lighting purchase plan includes lamps for:
    a. indoor fixtures.
    b. outdoor fixtures.
    c. hardwired fixtures.
    d. portable fixtures.
    e. All of the above

109. Which of the following are incorrect?
    a. LEED for Existing Buildings: Operation and Maintenance (LEED EB:O&M) addresses only the lamps purchased during the performance period, not the lamps installed in the building.
    b. LEED EB:O&M addresses not only the lamps purchased during the performance period, but also the lamps installed in the building.
    c. LEED EB:O&M requires that each purchased lamp comply with the specific mercury limit.
    d. LEED EB:O&M requires that only the overall average of purchased lamps must comply.

110. With regard to SS Credit: Light Pollution Reduction, one of the options for exterior lighting is to shield all exterior fixtures (where the sum of the mean lamp lumens for that fixture exceeds 2,500) such that the installed fixtures do not directly emit any light at a vertical angle more than ____ degrees from straight down.
   a. 60
   b. 70
   c. 80
   d. 90

111. Regarding EA Credit: Optimize Energy Performance, for buildings eligible to receive an energy performance rating using the EPA ENERGY STAR's Portfolio Manager tool, points are awarded for ENERGY STAR scores above _____.
   a. 50
   b. 65
   c. 75
   d. 85

112. What is the maximum number of points that a project team can earn under EA Credit: Optimize Energy Performance?
   a. 17
   b. 18
   c. 19
   d. 20

113. EA Prerequisite: Energy Efficiency Best Management Practices is related to which of the following? (Choose 2)
   a. SS Credit: Heat Island Reduction
   b. WE Credit: Indoor Water Use Reduction

c. EQ Credit: Indoor Air Quality Management Program
   d. EQ Credit: Green Cleaning—Custodial Effectiveness Assessment

114. Which building is not eligible for Energy Star Ratings?
   a. Factory
   b. Courthouse
   c. Hospital
   d. Warehouse

115. Regarding outdoor air monitoring for mechanically ventilated spaces under the EQ Credit: Enhanced Indoor Air Quality Strategies, a design team needs to provide a device capable of measuring the minimum outdoor airflow rate with an accuracy of within ± _____ of the design minimum outdoor air rate.
   a. 10%
   b. 15%
   c. 20%
   d. 25%

116. For a multifamily project seeking LEED EB:O&M certification, a project team needs to maintain a waste reduction and recycling program that reuses, recycles, or composts at least _____ of the durable goods waste as specified in the Materials and Resources Prerequisite: Ongoing Purchasing and Waste Policy (by weight, volume, or replacement value).
   a. 20%
   b. 40%

c. 50%
d. 75%

117. For EA Credit: Advanced Energy Metering, which of the following is not acceptable?
    a. Permanent metering and recording systems
    b. Metering and recording systems that operate continuously
    c. Metering and recording systems that operate automatically
    d. Metering and recording systems that operate electronically
    e. Manual metering reading

118. For EQ Credit: Green Cleaning—Products and Materials, general-purpose, bathroom, glass and carpet cleaners used for industrial and institutional purposes shall be certified by:
    a. "Green Label" testing program.
    b. "Green-e" testing program.
    c. "Seal of Approval program" testing program.
    d. EPA.

119. For a school project seeking LEED EB:O&M certification, with regard to WE Credit: Indoor Water Use Reduction, how many points can a project team earn if the indoor potable water use is reduced by 30%?
    a. 2
    b. 3
    c. 4
    d. 5

120. Which of the following is incorrect with regard to EA Credit: Existing Building Commissioning—Implementation?
    a. Implement low- or no-cost operations improvements.
    b. Implement all upgrades or retrofit for energy-using systems.
    c. Provide training for management staff.
    d. Update the building operating plan.

121. Which of the following are incorrect with regard to EA Credit: Ongoing Commissioning? (Choose 2)
    a. Only work completed within two years prior to application may be included to show progress in the ongoing commissioning cycle.
    b. Only work completed within one year prior to application may be included to show progress in the ongoing commissioning cycle.
    c. The ongoing commissioning plan includes roles and responsibilities.
    d. Ongoing commissioning is generally undertaken simultaneously with full retro-commissioning.

122. Which of the following can a project team use to show compliance with EQ Credit: Enhanced Indoor Air Quality Strategies? (Choose 2)
    a. Each ventilation system that supplies outdoor air to occupied spaces must have particle filters or air cleaning devices. These filters or devices must have a minimum efficiency reporting value (MERV) of 13 or

higher, in accordance with ASHRAE Standard 52.2–2007.
   b. Establish a regular schedule for maintenance and replacement of filtration media according to the manufacturer's recommended interval.
   c. CO2 monitors must be between 3 and 6 feet above the floor.
   d. CO2 monitors must be between 2 and 6 feet above the floor.

123. Which of the following can be exempt from the requirements of Carbon Dioxide Monitors for EQ Credit: Enhanced Indoor Air Quality Strategies? (Choose 2)
   a. Rooms smaller than 100 sf
   b. Rooms smaller than 150 sf
   c. If the total area of all naturally ventilated spaces is less than 5% of the area of the total occupied spaces
   d. Small conference rooms
   e. A Janitor's room

124. Wood products designated as FSC Recycled are:
   a. recycled content.
   b. recycled materials.
   c. diverted materials.
   d. FSC-certified wood.

125. How many levels of cleanliness do the APPA's Custodial Staffing Guidelines include?
   a. 3
   b. 4
   c. 5
   d. 6

126. For a multitenant building, a project seeking LEED EB:O&M certification must:
    a. involve a minimum of 90% of the total gross floor area
    b. involve a minimum of 90% of the total gross floor area and 90% of the tenant spaces
    c. involve a minimum of 80% of the total gross floor area
    d. involve a minimum of 80% of the total gross floor area and 80% of the tenant spaces

127. All of the following affect the targeted level of weighted average mercury content in lamps except: (Choose 2)
    a. colors.
    b. life span of lamps.
    c. lumen output.
    d. lamp types.

128. For LEED EB:O&M, the baseline water use is determined by:
    a. the year of substantial completion.
    b. the year when 100% of the building is completely finished.
    c. the year when the Certificate of Occupancy is issued.
    d. the year when at least 90% of the plumbing fixtures and fittings are retrofitted.

129. When calculating stormwater runoff volumes using the rational method, the following areas shall be included except:
    a. roof.
    b. pavement.
    c. surface waters.

d. turf.

130. With regard to MR Prerequisite: Facility Maintenance and Renovation Policy, what is the minimum MERV for the filtration media that a project uses for inside air recirculation and outside air intake?
    a. 8
    b. 13
    c. 15
    d. 17

131. Which of the following is not related to chemical management of the cooling tower?
    a. Bleed-off
    b. Condensation
    c. Biological control
    d. Staff management

132. What is EPA's I-BEAM related to?
    a. Integrated pest management
    b. Indoor Building Environment Air Management
    c. Emission reduction
    d. Light pollution reduction
    e. Indoor Air Quality Building Education and Assessment Model

133. A power company helps a project team build an on-site solar energy system and retains the environmental attributes. Which of the following is true?
    a. This solar system cannot earn points for EA Credit: Renewable Energy And Carbon Offsets
    b. The owner can use net-metering for this

system to earn credit.
c. This solar system can earn RECs.
d. None of the above

134. Visible light transmittance is related to which of the following?
    a. Albedo
    b. SRI
    c. Light pollution control
    d. Daylighting

135. Which of the following is not source reduction?
    a. Ordering the correct quantity and grade of concrete
    b. Protecting construction materials from weather damages
    c. Recycling extra gypsum boards
    d. Ordering the right quantity of equipment

136. With regard to EQ Credit: Enhanced Indoor Air Quality Strategies, the length of the building entrance grate system should be:
    a. 6 feet placed at the exterior of the building.
    b. 10 feet placed at the exterior of the building.
    c. 6 feet placed at the interior of the building.
    d. 10 feet placed at the interior of the building.

137. SS Credit: Site Management addresses the following except:
    a. calcium chloride or sodium chloride EPA deicers.
    b. air pollution from construction materials and activities.
    c. erosion and sedimentation control.
    d. diverting 80% of plant material waste via

low-impact means from landfills.

138. With regard to MR Credit: Purchasing—Ongoing, how much, by cost, of total ongoing consumables must meet at least one of the criteria listed in the performance section of the credit?
    a. 50%
    b. 60%
    c. 70%
    d. 80%

139. Which of the following are true regarding EQ Credit: Occupant Comfort Survey? (Choose 2)
    a. Administer at least one occupant a comfort survey.
    b. Administer at least two occupants comfort surveys.
    c. The responses must be collected from a representative sample of building occupants making up at least 30% of the total occupants.
    d. The responses must be collected from a representative sample of building occupants making up at least 80% of the total occupants.

140. What is bleed-off?
    a. It is the process of releasing a portion of the evaporating water from the cooling tower.
    b. It is the process of draining a portion of the re-circulating water from the cooling tower.
    c. It is the process of adding chemicals to the water used in the cooling tower.
    d. None of the above

141. What are the advantages of chemical treatment in cooling towers? (Choose 3)
    a. Reduction of potable water use
    b. Evaporation reduction
    c. Stronger cooling power
    d. Control of mineral deposits
    e. Prevention of legionella pneumophila outbreaks

142. With regard to WE Credit: Outdoor Water Use Reduction, a project team needs to demonstrate what percentage of a reduction in outdoor water use over the most recent 12 months compared with the established baseline to achieve 2 points under Performance, Option 3?
    a. 30%
    b. 40%
    c. 50%
    d. 60%

143. How can points be earned for WE Credit: Indoor Water Use Reduction?
    a. Have fixtures that use less water than the baseline calculated in WE Prerequisite Indoor Water-Use Reduction.
    b. Install sub-metering for at least 60% of the building area.
    c. Install sub-metering for at least 70% of the landscape area.
    d. Use ANSI irrigation performance and ranking tools to show compliance.

144. Which of the following is not related to WE Credit: Water Metering?
   a. Metering
   b. Sub-metering
   c. Process water
   d. Irrigation
   e. None of the above

145. Which of the following credit category is related to ENERGY STAR products?
   a. SS
   b. EA
   c. WE
   d. EQ

146. Which of the following can help earn SS Credit: Light Pollution Reduction?
   (Choose 2)
   a. Partially shield 60% of exterior light fixtures to prevent emitting light into the night sky.
   b. Partially shield all exterior light fixtures to prevent emitting light into the night sky.
   c. Measure the night illumination levels at regularly spaced points on the project boundary.
   d. All exterior light fixtures should be at least 30% partially shielded to prevent light emittance into the night sky.
   e. Install a monitoring system.

147. Which of the following are not required to earn EA Credit: Ongoing Commissioning? (Choose 2)
   a. Develop an on-going commissioning plan.
   b. Complete 100% of the scope of the work before submitting the application for LEED EB:O&M.

c. Use only actual costs to document completed tasks.
d. Apply the credit requirements to all direct energy-consuming or energy-producing systems.

148. Which of the following are not related to Building Automation System (BAS)? (Choose 2)
    a. DDC
    b. Occupancy sensors
    c. Controlled devices
    d. Time clock
    e. Setpoints and setbacks

149. How many point(s) will a project earn if it has in place an Environmentally Preferable Purchasing (EPP) Policy?
    a. 0
    b. 1
    c. 2
    d. 3

150. In an office building where the tenant turn-over rate is high, what is the best sustainable strategy?
    a. A furniture salvage program
    b. Selling used furniture to recycled facilities
    c. Buying only furniture with pre- and postconsumer content
    d. RECs
    e. Green Seal program

151. All typical HVAC equipment is assumed to have a life of:
    a. 10 years
    b. 15 years

c. 20 years
d. 25 years
e. 30 years

152. What is the maximum number of points that a project can earn for exemplary performance under IOc1: Innovation in Operations?
    a. 2
    b. 3
    c. 4
    d. 5

153. A project team must document the following in writing for Option 1. Innovation under IN Credit: Innovation except: (Choose 3)
    a. intent.
    b. definition.
    c. strategies.
    d. performance metric.
    e. reference codes.

154. With regard to EA Credit: Existing Building Commissioning—Implementation, which of the following changes will affect building operating plan updates? (Choose 3)
    a. Lighting level
    b. Equipment run-time schedule
    c. Sustainable purchase
    d. Occupancy schedule
    e. Solid waste management

155. If a project is certified under LEED EB:O&M, how often can the project be recertified?
    a. Every year
    b. Every two years
    c. Every three years

d. Every four years
   e. Every five years

156. What is the maximum "gap" within a performance period?
   a. one day
   b. one week
   c. one month
   d. one year

157. With regard to EQ Credit: Occupant Comfort Survey, what percentage of occupants must be included in the occupant comfort survey?
   a. 30%
   b. 60%
   c. 80%
   d. 90%

158. Which of the following are not a type of structural control for controlling erosion and sedimentation? (Choose 2)
   a. Silt fencing
   b. Mulching
   c. Catch basin
   d. Earth dike

159. Which of the following are not types of non-potable water that can be used for WE Credit: Cooling Tower Water Use? (Choose 2)
   a. Swimming pool filter backwash water
   b. Recycled treated wastewater from toilet and urinal flushing
   c. Naturally occurring groundwater
   d. Surface water

160. An operations and maintenance plan is also called:
    a. owner's operating requirements.
    b. developer's operating requirements.
    c. tenant's operating requirements.
    d. management's operating requirements.

161. With regard to a cooling tower, which of the following can help to prevent exposure to Legionella pneumophila? (Choose 2)
    a. The use of non-potable water
    b. Biocides
    c. Reducing evaporation
    d. Well-maintained drift eliminators
    e. The use of potable water

162. With regard to EA Credit: Optimize Energy Performance, for buildings eligible to receive an energy performance rating using the EPA ENERGY STAR's Portfolio Manager tool, points are awarded for ENERGY STAR scores above_____?
    a. 50
    b. 55
    c. 65
    d. 75
    e. 85

163. What is the minimum initial performance period for LEED EB:O&M?
    a. 1 month
    b. 3 months
    c. 6 months
    d. 9 months
    e. 12 months
    f. 24 months

164. What is the maximum performance period?
    a. 9 months
    b. 12 months
    c. 24 months
    d. 36 months

165. For stormwater quantity control, a project team needs to perform all necessary stabilization, repairs, or routine required maintenance within __days of inspection?
    a. 15
    b. 30
    c. 45
    d. 60

166. For a naturally ventilated space, which of the following is not an acceptable way to meet the requirements of EQ Credit: Enhanced Indoor Air Quality Strategies?
    a. Provide a direct exhaust airflow measurement device capable of measuring the exhaust airflow.
    b. Provide an alarm that indicates when airflow values vary by 15% or more from the exhaust airflow setpoint.
    c. Calibrate all measurement devices within the manufacturer's recommended interval.
    d. None of the above

167. A project team has conducted a walk-through analysis two years before the performance period. Which of the following are true with regard to EA Prerequisite: Energy Efficiency Best Management Practices? (Choose 2)
    a. The project team has to redo the walk-

through analysis again.
b. The project team does not have to redo the walk-through analysis again.
c. The project team has to do an updated report.
d. None of the above

168. Which of the following belong to operational effective credits? (Choose 2)
a. Metering of energy use
b. Non-potable water use
c. Pest management methods
d. Optimizing daylight and views

169. A $100 purchase that contains 60%, by cost, of total ongoing consumables that are postconsumer recycled content can be counted as _____ of sustainable purchasing?
a. $100
b. $150
c. $200
d. $300

170. How can a multifamily project seeking LEED EB:O&M certification meet EQ Prerequisite: Minimum Indoor Air Quality Performance? (Choose 2)
a. Meet ASHRAE 62.1-2010.
b. Meet ASHRAE 90.1-2010.
c. International projects may instead meet the alternative minimum outdoor air requirements.
d. Supply at least 20 cubic feet per minute per person of outdoor air.

171. Which of the following are not the I-BEAM protocols for managing major sources of pollution in buildings? (Choose 2)
    a. Shipping and receiving
    b. Using filters with proper MERV
    c. Pest control
    d. Entry grates with sufficient length
    e. Painting
    f. Remodeling and renovation

172. Which of the following are strategies for promoting hand hygiene and compliance with green cleaning policy? (Choose 2)
    a. Use hand soaps with antimicrobial agents if allowed by codes.
    b. Use hand soaps without antimicrobial agents if allowed by codes.
    c. Use hand paper towels with recycled content.
    d. Use waterless hand sanitizers.

173. A project team has done an O+M Occupant Commute Survey, and only 70% of the regular building occupants responded. Which of the following is true?
    a. This survey is not valid because it has not reached the minimum percentage required.
    b. The non-respondents are considered as solo drivers.
    c. The project can extrapolate the commuting behavior of the respondents to non-respondents.
    d. None of the above

174. With regard to EA Credit: Advanced Energy Metering, how often must the project team report the facility's utility peak demand and total consumption?
   a. Weekly
   b. Monthly
   c. Quarterly
   d. Yearly

175. With regard to light pollution reduction, if the top of a window glass is 8 feet from the floor, what is the exempt distance from the window for an interior light that is above the top of the window glass?
   a. 4 feet
   b. 8 feet
   c. 12 feet
   d. 16 feet

176. With regard to the building exterior and hardscape management plan, which of the following are less environmentally friendly ways of snow and ice removal? (Choose 2)
   a. Calcium chloride
   b. Magnesium chloride
   c. Potassium acetate
   d. Sodium chloride

177. How should the energy-use intensity be calculated?
   a. Total kBtu/Gross Floor Area
   b. Total kw/Gross Floor Area
   c. Total Energy Cost/Gross Floor Area
   d. (Total Energy Cost + Total Water Cost)/Gross Floor Area

178. What is the intent of ASHRAE Level walk-through?
    a. To conduct an energy audit
    b. To check and adjust BAS
    c. To check and adjust the lighting system
    d. To check and adjust the HVAC system

179. If a project is not eligible for an Energy Star Rating, it must be ____ more energy efficient than the average of similar types of buildings in the nation to qualify for LEED EB:O&M certification.
    a. 25%
    b. 23%
    c. 21%
    d. 19%

180. Which of the following lists each distinct type of system, such as humidification, dehumidification, ventilation, space cooling, etc.?
    a. Building operating plan
    b. Preventive maintenance plan
    c. Sequence of operations
    d. Systems narrative

181. Which of the following are ineligible on-site renewable systems? (Choose 3)
    a. Photovoltaic
    b. Passive solar strategies
    c. Animal waste
    d. Landfill gas
    e. Daylighting strategies
    f. Geoexchange systems

182. How many points can a project seeking LEED EB:O&M certification earn for exemplary performance under IN Credit: Innovation?
    a. 1
    b. 2
    c. 3
    d. 4

183. How many points can a project seeking LEED EB:O&M certification earn for RP Credit: Regional Priority?
    a. 3
    b. 4
    c. 5
    d. 6

184. If a project's site area is 1 acre and the building footprint is 10,000 sf, how much of the site area needs to be covered with adapted or native plants for the project to earn 2 points for SS Credit: Site Development—Protect Or Restore Habitat?
    a. 2,536 sf
    b. 5,018 sf
    c. 7,532 sf
    d. 8,712 sf

185. What is the CIBSE Application Manual related to?
    a. BMP
    b. Energy audit
    c. Air conditioning
    d. Ventilation
    e. Lighting

186. Which of the following must a detailed plan for ongoing commissioning include? (Choose 3)
   a. Maintenance tasks
   b. Measurement requirements
   c. Operation schedule
   d. Review process
   e. Frequency of analyses

187. Which of the following are true? (Choose 2)
   a. A project must have an Energy Star Rating of 71 or higher to earn an Energy Star Label.
   b. A project must have an Energy Star Rating of 75 or higher to earn an Energy Star Label.
   c. A project that is not eligible for an Energy Star Label can earn LEED certification.
   d. A project that is not eligible for an Energy Star Label cannot earn LEED certification.

188. In an unincorporated area with no codes regarding erosion control, which of the following shall a project team follow?
   a. CPESC
   b. EPA's Stormwater Pollution Prevention Plans
   c. IPM
   d. Erosion Control Technical Council

189. With regard to LT Credit: Alternative Transportation, Alternative Commuting Transportation includes all but which of the following?
   a. Human-powered conveyances
   b. Alternative-fuel vehicle
   c. Expanded workweeks
   d. Telecommuting

190. A vegetated roof can contribute to all but which of the following?
    a. SS Credit: Heat Island Reduction
    b. EA Credit: Optimize Energy Performance
    c. EQ Credit: Daylight and Quality Views
    d. SS Credit: Site Development—Protect or Restore Habitat

191. Which of the following is related to an ASHRAE Level 2 Energy Audit?
    a. EA Prerequisite: Energy Efficiency Best Management Practices
    b. EA Credit: Optimize Energy Performance
    c. EA CREDIT: Existing Building Commissioning—Analysis
    d. EA Prerequisite: Building-Level Energy Metering

192. Which of the following tasks is not included in an ASHRAE Level 2 Energy Audit?
    a. A rough estimate energy-use breakdown per 1996 ASHRAE Handbook
    b. A review of the electrical and mechanical system design
    c. A list of possible modifications that can save money
    d. An estimate of the cost for each practical measure

193. Excluding skylights, photovoltaic panels, and mechanical equipment, which of the following will help a project earn an IN Credit: Innovation Exemplary Performance point?
    a. A vegetated roof that covers 95% of the roof area

b. A vegetated roof that covers 75% of the roof area
c. (Area of Roof Meeting Minimum SRI/Total Roof Area) x (SRI of Installed Roof/Required SRI)≥75%
d. (Area of Roof Meeting Minimum SRI/0.75) x (SRI of Installed Roof/0.5)≥ Total Roof Area

194. With regard to SS Credit: LEED Certified Design and Construction, which of the following is true?
    a. If the project has been certified under LEED NC before, it can earn 3 points.
    b. If the project has been certified under LEED School before, it can earn 2 points.
    c. If the project has been certified under LEED CS and 75% of the floor area has been certified under LEED CI before, it can earn an IO bonus point.
    d. If the project has been certified under LEED CS and 75% of the floor area has been certified under LEED CI before, it can earn 4 points.
    e. None of the above.

195. Per Energy Star Rating System, what is an average building's performance?
    a. 21
    b. 45
    c. 50
    d. 71

196. With regard to the EA Credit: Ongoing Commissioning, only work completed within __ _____ years prior to application may be included to show progress in the ongoing commissioning cycle
   a. two
   b. three
   c. four
   d. five

197. With regard to SS Credit: Light Pollution Reduction, which of the following can help a project to earn one point?
   a. All non-emergency lights visible from outside must be programmed to automatically turn off for at least 50% of the nighttime hours every night.
   b. The project must have earned LEED NC certification and at least 75% of the total floor area must have been certified under LEED CI.
   c. Shield exterior fixtures to prevent them from emitting any light at certain angle.
   d. The exterior lighting level must be equal to 20% or less of the interior lighting level.

198. With regard to MR Credit: Purchasing—Facility Maintenance and Renovation, which of the following standards must the exterior sealant comply with?
   a. SCAQMD
   b. Green Seal's Standard GS-11
   c. Environmental Choice CCD-110
   d. SMACNA

199. A project team is seeking an Energy Star Rating for a building, EPA allows the exclusion of up to 10% of gross floor area if: (Choose 2)
   a. the space does not fit any of the Energy Star space type classifications.
   b. the energy use of that space is estimated accurately based on similar spaces.
   c. the energy use of that space is submetered.
   d. the space is completely sealed off and separated from other spaces.

200. A project team can use _____ to relate the emissions from a building's energy consumption to the source of that energy.
   a. NERC Regions
   b. eGRID Subregions
   c. Portfolio Managers
   d. Energy Star's Portfolio Manager

201. Which of the following cannot earn exemplary performance points?
   a. SS Credit: Rainwater Management
   b. SS Credit: Heat Island Reduction
   c. SS Credit: Site Development—Protect or Restore Habitat
   d. SS Credit: Light Pollution Reduction

Chapter Two
LEED AP O+M Exam Mock Exam Answers and Explanations (Including Both Part One and Part Two)

I. Answers and Explanations for the LEED AP O+M Mock Exam Part One

If you answer 80 of the 100 questions correctly for a section, you have passed the mock exam for that section.

1. Answer: a
   The MEP Engineer has the most influence in energy performance, and the credit, Optimize Energy Performance.

2. Answer: a, c, and e
   The project team should include the following as part of **process energy**:
   Refrigeration and kitchen cooking, laundry (washing and drying), elevators and escalators, computers, office and general miscellaneous equipment, lighting not included in the lighting power allowance (such as lighting that is part of the medical equipment), and other uses like water

pumps, etc.

3. Answer: a, c, and d
   The project team should include the following as **regulated (non-process) energy**:
   HVAC, exhaust fans and hoods, lighting for interiors, surface parking, garage parking, building façade and grounds, space heating, and service water heating, etc.

4. Answer: a and b
   Points for the WE category:
   a. LEED BDC NC: 11 points
   b. LEED BDC CS: 11 points
   c. LEED BDC Schools: 12 points
   d. LEED IDC CI: 12 points
   e. LEED OM EB: 12 points

5. Answer: a
   Buildings codes, ADA, Municipal codes, and EPA Codes of Federal Regulations are laws, because they have gone through the legislation process, but reference guides by USGBC are NOT laws. They are rules set by the USGBC and have NO legal authority like the other governing agencies.

   LEED standards are voluntary. You choose to obey the rules when you seek certification for a building, but these rules are NOT laws.

6. Answer: a and c
   The manufacture of HVAC units containing CFCs was stopped in the United States in 1995. These units had been phased out from existing buildings located in the United States by 2011.

7. Answer: c, d, and e
   Increasing the site coverage or FAR will increase impervious area and will increase stormwater runoff. Porous pavement will help recharge the groundwater thereby reducing stormwater runoff, and high-albedo (high-reflectivity) materials will increase reflectivity to alleviate the urban "heat island" effect. Vegetated roofs and retention ponds can also reduce stormwater runoff and alleviate the urban "heat island" effect.

8. Answer: b
   Recycled materials can protect virgin materials, but may require more energy to process, can increase traffic, and increase MEP cost.

9. Answer: f
   Graywater is the household water that has not come into contact with the kitchen sink or toilet waste.

   See USGBC Definitions at the following link: https://www.usgbc.org/ShowFile.aspx?DocumentID=5744

   The definitions on the PDF file that you can download from the link above should be read at least three times. Become very familiar with them and MEMORIZE. LEED exams always test these definitions.

10. Answer: c and d
    Blackwater, otherwise known as **brown water**,

foul water, or sewage, is water from the kitchen sink, dishwasher, or water that has come into contact with human or animal waste.

11. Answer: a and d
    Read the question carefully; it is asking for the WRONG statements.

12. Answer: b and d
    Both the Uniform Plumbing Code (**UPC**) and International Plumbing Code (**IPC**) set standards for plumbing fixture water use, and their requirements for the water use baseline are the same in many cases.

13. Answer: a
    This question tests your knowledge of the Energy Policy Act (EPAct) of 1992. Although called the Energy Policy Act, it deals with water savings. This is the trick.

14. Answer: d
    MPRs include some very basic requirements. For example:
    1) The building must be 1,000 sf minimum for LEED BDC NC, LEED BDC Schools, LEED BDC CS, and LEED EB:O&M. There is a 250 sf minimum for LEED IDC CI.
    2) The building to site ratio must be 2% or higher. 2% x 200,000 sf = 4,000 sf

15. Answer: b
    The maximum number of Regional Priority points a project can achieve is 4 out of the 6 possible points. A project team needs to select which 4 of the 6 points to use.

16. Answer: d
    The LEED O&M rating system deals with buildings after construction is completed. All other answers are not unique to LEED O&M.

17. Answer: a
    You should use the definition of a renewable source given by the Center for Resource Solution's (CRS) in their Green-e product requirements to determine which power to purchase. The question is asking for a program, not an organization. Center for Resource Solution's (CRS) is an organization, while Green-e is a program.

18. Answer: b
    Both albedo and SRI are good indexes, but SRI is the better option. SRI stands for Solar Reflectance Index.

19. Answer: c and e
    Pay attention to the word "not" in the question.

20. Answer: a
    When you recycle, materials are sent to recycling facilities.

21. Answer: d
    LEED is a system set up by USGBC, and not by the federal government or International Code Council (ICC). USGBC is NOT a government agency. Building codes and green building codes are set up by the local government per the ICC model codes.

For LEED, water savings are based on the percentage of water saved by the design case when compared with a baseline building.

22. Answer: c
Community connectivity is the best answer. The other answers have some merit, but they are not the best answer.

23. Answer: a
Community connectivity is the best answer. All other answers are distracters to confuse you. If you have a firm knowledge of community connectivity, you should be able to answer this question correctly.

24. Answer: a
Open spaces need to be vegetated and pervious areas. Areas under canopy and atriums with views to the ocean are typically not considered open spaces for a LEED project.

25. Answer: b
Pay attention to the word "except" in the question. LEED certification does NOT involve extra time or effort for a city's plan check or permitting.

26. Answer: c
For planning a project's LEED certification, the earlier this is done in the process, the better.

27. Answer: d
You cannot include a shared parking structure on an adjacent property as part of the project area, because it belongs to someone other than your

project owner.
28. Answer: d
You cannot use CFC-refrigerant in new buildings. LEED NC is a rating system for new buildings.

29. Answer: c
Green-e product requirements written by the Center for Resource Solutions are used as guidelines for purchasing your building's electricity from off-site renewable sources. The purchase is based on quantity, NOT the cost, and contracts for this renewable energy should be at least five years long.

30. Answer: a and c
Only vehicles classified as **Zero Emission Vehicles (ZEV)** by California Air Resources Board or vehicles with a green score of at least 45 on the **American Council for an Energy Efficient Economy (ACEEE)** annual vehicle rating guide are qualified as fuel efficient and low emitting vehicles for LEED credit.

31. Answer: b
The manufacture of HVAC units containing CFCs was stopped in the United States in 1995. These units had been phased out from existing U.S. buildings by 2011. Halons are used for fire suppression systems, NOT HVAC systems. Dry ice is commonly used to preserve food, instead of being used as HVAC refrigerant.

32. Answer: b
Per UPC, **graywater** is the household water that has not come into contact with the kitchen sink or

toilet waste.

33. Answer: a and c
Halons cause damage to the ozone layer, but a building using a halon-based fire suppression system can still seek LEED certification. This building must meet Fire Department requirements concerning halons.

34. Answer: d
Answers "a" and "b" have some merit, but they are not the fundamental cause of global warming. The rest of the answers are simply distracters.

35. Answer: c
The <u>Sheet Metal and Air Conditioning National Contractors Association (SMACNA)</u> has an IAQ Guideline for Occupied Buildings Under Construction.

36. Answer: a, b, and c
American Council for an Energy Efficient Economy (ACEEE) and Tradable Renewable Certificates (TRCs) are universal and not local issues.

37. Answer: a and d
Please note that we are looking for statements that are <u>NOT</u> true. Bicycle racks will <u>NOT</u> help community connectivity. Retention ponds will reduce stormwater runoff.

38. Answer: b
A construction waste management plan should include materials to be used for alternative daily cover (ADC). Answers "c" and "d" should be part

of the design phase decisions. The recycling capacity of the neighborhood recycle center does NOT need to be part of the construction waste management plan.

39. Answer: c and d
Using the system that can gain the most points for LEED makes sense, but is not mandated by USGBC. Asking a landlord for advice is not a good choice and is NOT professional; the project team should be the advisor for the landlord. Using the 40/60 rule is correct. The **40/60 rule for LEED**: if a LEED system applies to 40% or less of the project or spaces, do not use it; if a LEED system applies to 60% or more of the project or spaces, use it. In the end, the project team makes an independent and final decision.

See "LEED Rating System Selection Policy" at the link below:

http://www.usgbc.org/docs/archive/general/docs 10132.pdf

Read this free document at least three times, because it is very important, and explains when to use each LEED system.

40. Answer: a
The project team cannot seek precertification as a marketing tool for funding and attracting tenants, because precertification is for the LEED BDC CS (Core and Shell) rating system or LEED Volume Program ONLY. If the project has a signed lease or LOI for at least 70% of the spaces, this is good,

but NOT required by GBCI. GBCI also does NOT require the project to be located in a new neighborhood for LEED NC.

41. Answer: c

    The project team can gain a point under IN because this program provides <u>quantitative</u> performance improvements for environmental benefit, which is <u>substantially</u> better than typical sustainable practice, and is applicable to <u>other</u> projects. Answer "b" is incorrect because the recycling credit for MR involves the building occupants (not the general public), and is limited to the following materials only:

    <u>P</u>aper
    <u>C</u>ardboard
    <u>M</u>etal
    <u>G</u>lass
    <u>P</u>lastics

    Mnemonics: People <u>C</u>an <u>M</u>ake <u>G</u>reen <u>P</u>romises

42. Answer: c, d, and e

    Wind and biofuel are clean energy. Natural gas is pretty clean, but still generates air pollution.

43. Answer: b and d

    Using water efficient fixtures applies only to indoor water; using native plants applies only to outdoor water; using sub-meters can monitor water leakage, and applies to all three cases. Water saving education programs can help teach all building users to save water, and applies to all three cases as well.

44. Answer: c
    ROI is a return on investment; **life-cycle analysis** is used to analyze the environmental impact of a building over its lifetime; **life-cycle cost analysis** is used to analyze the cost/savings of a building over its lifetime; life-cycle saving analysis is a distracter, and this term does not exist.

45. Answer: a
    ASHRAE 55-2010 includes standards regarding major factors affecting human comfort, such as temperature, humidity, air speed, etc. **ASHRAE 62.1-2010** is related to natural ventilation; the Carpet and Rug Institute's **Green Label Plus** program is in regards to carpet and rugs; Green Building Index is a sustainable building rating tool used in Malaysia.

46. Answer: d
    If you pass the LEED Green Associate Exam, you can use the LEED Green Associate title or logo per GBCI guidelines on your business card. This question is testing your knowledge about the different scope of work done by GBCI and USGBC, and the proper use of the LEED Green Associate title or logo. Per GBCI, LEED GA is never an approved abbreviation of the LEED Green Associate title or logo.

    I use LEED GA as part of this book's main title simply because it is more legible on Amazon.com than using the full LEED Green Associate title.

47. Answer: d
    Furniture containing VOCs will affect EQ. The "450 miles from the job site" is included as a distracter.

48. Answer: d
    Green building through a <u>holistic</u> design approach has no <u>definite</u> relationship to construction time, cost, or savings over a building's lifetime. The design approach does improve the <u>synergy</u> of LEED credits.

49. Answer: c
    The building's foot print = the first floor area = 168,000 sf/8 = 21,000 sf

50. Answer: a
    1 acre = 43,560 sf. The site coverage = the first floor area/site area = 21,000/43,560 = 48%. This question tests your basic construction knowledge: 1 acre = 43,560 sf and the concept of site coverage.

51. Answer: b
    FAR (Floor Area Ratio) = the total building area/total **buildable** site area = 168,000/43,560 = 386%. This question tests your basic construction knowledge: 1 acre = 43,560 sf.

    This question also tests your knowledge of USGBC's definition of FAR which is TOTALLY different from what we are used to in the construction industry. I think this one will throw many people off. It's a good trick.

See USGBC Definitions at the link below: https://www.usgbc.org/ShowFile.aspx?DocumentID=5744

52. Answer: c
    For a single building project, the perimeter of the LEED project is typically the project's boundary; for a multi-building project, the LEED project team can choose a portion of the project site to submit as the LEED project boundary.

53. Answer: d
    Green roofs include vegetated roofs and light color reflective roofs. Light color reflective roofs are NOT landscape areas. Retention ponds and sidewalks are not considered landscape areas. The best answer is vegetated roofs.

54. Answer: b. ASHRAE Standard 55-2010
    ASHRAE 62.1-2010 relates to both EQ and EA category. The other two standards relate to LEED EA category only.

55. Answer: c
    All the other answers are hard costs (material costs).

56. Answer: c
    USGBC is in charge of creating all reference guides and the related errata.

57. Answer: c
    Pay attention to the word "typically."

58. Answer: a
Technical Advisory Group is the best answer. The LEED Administrator is a distracter. USGBC is no longer involved with building LEED certification. GBCI depends on the Technical Advisory Group for CIRs.

59. Answer: b
ASHRAE 62.1-2010 specifies minimum ventilation rates for IAQ Performance. See EAP: Minimum Energy Performance.

60. Answer: a
ASTM and USGBC do not publish GWP and ODP scores. The Global Climate Control Board does not exist.

61. Answer: c
Universal Energy Conservation Codes and Energy Rating Codes do not exist. IPC stands for International Plumbing Code.

62. Answer: c
High SRI value and albedo can help alleviate the heat island effect. Adding trees to a parking lot can reduce stormwater runoff to some extent, but grouping buildings together can reduce the hardscape areas, and is the most effective way to reduce stormwater runoff.

63. Answer: d
The qualified Basic Services that can help to gain LEED points for community connectivity include, but are not limited to:
a) Place of Worship

b) Restaurant
c) Supermarket
d) Convenience Grocery
e) Laundry
f) Cleaner
g) Beauty Salon
h) Hardware
i) Pharmacy
j) Medical/Dental
k) Bank
l) Senior Care Facility
m) Community Center
n) Fitness Center
o) Daycare
p) School
q) Library
r) Museum
s) Theater
t) Park
u) Fire Station
v) Post Office

A shopping center includes many of the basic services listed above, and is the best choice.

64. Answer: c
    A car powered by gas is a non-alternative-fuel vehicle

65. Answer: d
    Answer "a" is considered carpooling; Answer "b" is simply sharing parking cost; and Answer "c" is a shuttle service program.

66. Answer: a

A project team does NOT need to certify everything inside the property boundary, and can determine the LEED project site boundary for LEED submittal and certification.

67. Answer: b
Per UPC, **graywater** is household water that has not come into contact with kitchen sinks, human excretion, or animal waste. Graywater includes used water from bathroom washbasins, bathtubs, showers, and water from laundry tubs and clothes washers. Graywater does not include water from dishwashers or kitchen sinks.

68. Answer: c
Cradle-to-cradle analysis is the same as life cycle analysis, eco-balance, or life cycle assessment, and is used to evaluate the environmental impact of a service or product. We use whole building perspective for LEED. Energy reduction is only one aspect of LEED. LEED includes other categories, such as SS, WE, EQ, etc. Integrated design approach is a design approach that includes consideration for people, planet and profit (triple bottom line or three Ps).

69. Answer: a
CFC can be replaced with CO_2 or other refrigerants. Halons are used for fire suppression systems. The manufacture of HVAC units containing CFCs was stopped in the United States in 1995. These units had been phased out from existing buildings located in the United States by 2011.

70. Answer: a and e
    SRI stands for Solar Reflectance Index. Albedo means solar reflectance.

71. Answer: b
    RECs mean Renewable Energy Certificates. They represent positive attributes of power generated by renewable sources. When you purchase RECs, you are buying the attributes, NOT necessarily the real power used in your project. Anyone can purchase RECs from anywhere, even if the power used in his/her project is not green power. The money s/he pays allows others to generate or use green power, and achieves overall reduction of the use of fossil fuels in the world. This is a marketing approach for sustainability.

72. Answer: b and d
    Per USGBC, the priorities for LEED projects are based on environmental guidelines and project constraints.

73. Answer: c
    Burning construction waste on site is not acceptable. Answers "a" and "b" are good practice, but they cannot reduce construction waste.

74. Answer: d
    Prerequisites and credits are part of the LEED building rating systems, MPRs are Minimum Project Requirements, and the foundation of the LEED building rating systems is the triple bottom line, which means people, profit, and

planet.

75. Answer: c
    The project cannot use LEED BDC NC certification because the building is less than 9 stories high. The project team should use the LEED BD+C: Homes and Multifamily Lowrise rating system instead.

76. Answer: d
    Per Montreal Protocol, the manufacture of HVAC units containing CFCs was stopped in the United States in 1995. These units had been phased out from existing buildings located in the United States by 2011. HCFCs, which are less active, have to be phased out by 2030.

77. Answer: b and c
    Grease typically goes down the drains in the kitchen as part of the blackwater. Toxic metal can be found in blackwater also. CO and halons are unlikely to be found in wastewater.

78. Answer: c
    Answer "a" is good practice, but is not the best choice; no matter how good a job you do, the system can still fail and leak out refrigerants. Answer "b" is partially correct; there are refrigerants without ODP (ozone depletion potential) that still have GWP (global warming potential). Answer "c" is the best choice; if you do not use refrigerants, there is absolutely no chance for them to leak out and cause environmental damage.

79. Answer: a and d
    The LEED project boundary only includes the portion of the site submitted by the project team for LEED certification, and does not necessarily overlap with the edge of the entire development, or the edge of the building. The boundary does include the entire project scope of work

80. Answer: b and d
    Reduced disturbance of wetlands is an environmental benefit, not necessarily an economic benefit. Increased use of rapidly renewable materials may not save money. Better EQ does create fewer liabilities, lowers the cost related to employees' health, and reduces the number of employee sick days.

81. Answer: c and d
    Biofuel is generated from plant material like crops, trees, and grasses. Gas and natural gas are both fossil fuels.

82. Answer: a
    All other choices are good practice, but they do NOT necessarily need to be implemented for water efficiency.

83. Answer: a
    This is the definition of durability.

84. Answer: b and c
    The removal of refrigerants containing ODP and GWP should be conducted by a specialist, and is not part of a construction waste management

plan. The reduction of building size is part of the design decision, not part of a construction waste management plan.

85. Answer: c and d
HCFCS and CFCs should not be used because of their ozone depletion potential (ODP).

86. Answer: b and d
Both answer "b" and "d" can earn points for Innovation.

87. Answer: c
The same strategy can be used for other projects, but it may or may not earn an IN point. Each case has to be reviewed and determined by GBCI.

88. Answer: b
NH3 has a lower GWP than HCFC.

For more information see: "**The Treatment by LEED of the Environmental Impact of HVAC Refrigerants**." You can download this PDF file for free at the link below:

http://www.gbci.org/Files/References/The-Treatment-by-LEED-of-the-Environmental-Impact-of-HVAC-Refrigerants.pdf

This is a VERY important document that you need to become familiar with. Many real LEED exam questions (CFC, HCFC, HFC, etc.) come from this document. You should download the file and read at least 3 times.

Pay special attention to the Table on ODP and GWP. You do not have to remember the exact value of all ODPs and GWPs, but you do need to know the rough number for various groups of refrigerants.

89. Answer: a and c
An educational program on LEED is the most common way to gain points under the Innovation category. Answer "c" may earn extra points for Exemplary Performance under the Innovation category. Answer "b" may help the project earn a higher level of LEED certification, but no other rewards.

90. Answer: a
Proper building orientation and fenestration can take full advantage of the dominant winds in the summer, and avoid chilly north winds in the winter. These characteristics can also take full advantage of passive heating from the sun in the winter, and avoid the westerly sun in the summer. This can be more efficient than ALL the HVAC equipment combined. There is no such thing as LEED certified equipment.

91. Answer: c
All LEED rating systems can have CIRs, including LEED ND.

92. Answer: b
ASHRAE standards do not apply to WE.

93. Answer: b
Rainwater is non-potable water. Please also see

the definitions for blackwater and graywater in the explanations of Questions #9, #10, #32, and #67. Raw water is a distracter.

94. Answer: b
Prerequisites are the most important criteria for a LEED building rating system. They HAVE to be met before a building can earn LEED certification. Quantifiable performances, credits, and third party standards only apply to part of the LEED rating systems, and not ALL of them have to be met.

95. Answer: b and d
Hardscape can reduce landscape area; mulches can prevent moisture loss. Both can reduce water for landscape irrigation. Perennials use more water. Overhead irrigation can increase water loss due to runoff and evaporation by the sun and wind. Head to head coverage is a standard practice for landscape irrigation.

96. Answer: a and d
The following is true with regard to SSC: Heat Island Reduction? (Choose 2)
- Temperatures in urban areas can be 22°F (12°C) higher than undeveloped areas and surrounding suburbs.
- Measures to reduce heat islands measures include using a vegetated roof to insulate a building and extend the life of the roof or installing solar panels or shading devices.

Urban heat islands contribute to 24.2% (*not* 38.2. You do not need to memorize the exact percentage, but need to have a general idea) of regional warming according to a study of surface warming caused by rapid urbanization in east China.

The **solar reflectance index (SRI)** is the most effective measure of the ability of roofing materials to reject solar heat. However, in this credit, **solar reflectance (SR,** *not* SRI) is used to measure the solar heat rejection of "non-roof" materials or components that are not considered roofing materials, such as shading devices, vegetation, and other less reflective components.

97. Answer: d
Lightweight plants are most appropriate for a vegetated roof. Native plants or adaptive plants are good for LEED projects, but some of them are NOT appropriate for rooftops. A native tree with a large canopy on a vegetated roof means large roots will be present and may cause many problems.

98. Answer: b, d, and e
Consultation with an electrical engineer is good practice, but it is not as important as the other choices. The completion of the commissioning plan will occur AFTER onsite renewable systems are selected.

99. Answer: c
Scraps re-used from the same manufacture process, such as reground and rework, cannot be included as pre-consumer recycled items or post-consumer recycled items. Therefore, Answers "a" and "d" are incorrect. Demolition

concrete pieces used at another project are salvaged materials.

100. Answer: e

The project team can ONLY advise the school board that the LEED Platinum certification is achieved after the LEED application is reviewed and APPROVED by GBCI, because the GBCI can reject the application after the review or approve the project for a lower level of LEED certification.

II. Answers and Explanations for the LEED AP O+M Mock Exam Part Two

If you answer 80 of the 100 questions correctly for a section, you have passed the mock exam for that section.

101. Answer: c
 LEED O+M includes 7 categories of certification:
 LEED O+M: Existing Buildings
 LEED O+M: Schools
 LEED O+M: Retails
 LEED O+M: Data Centers
 LEED O+M: Hospitality
 LEED O+M: Warehouse and Distribution Centers
 LEED O+M: Multifamily

102. Answer: d
 LEED O+M includes 8 credit categories:
 Location and Transportation (LT)
 Sustainable Sites (SS)
 Water Efficiency (WE)
 Energy and Atmosphere (EA)
 Materials and Resources (MR)
 Indoor Environmental Quality (EQ)
 Innovation (IN)
 Regional Priority (RP)

103. Answer: b
 For a retail building seeking LEED EB:O&M certification, to gain 2 points for WE Credit: Outdoor Water Use Reduction, a project team needs to reduce water use by 40%.

According to WE Credit: Outdoor Water Use Reduction, EB: O&M, Performance, Option 3, Irrigation Meter Installed (1–2 points), Demonstrating a 40% reduction in outdoor water use over the most recent 12 months compared with the established baseline will help the project team to gain 2 points.

104. Answer: d
Having a green cleaning policy in place is a prerequisite for projects seeking LEED EB:O&M certification. It is mandatory but will not help a project team achieve any points.
See EQ Prerequisite: Green Cleaning Policy.

105. Answer: a
Pay attention to the word "except" in the question.

Choice "a" missed a critical word: "no." The correct statement should be:

Use *no* calcium chloride or sodium chloride deicers, and/or establish reduced treatment areas equal to 50% of applicable paving area.

106. Answer: b and d

Please note that we are looking for statements are not true

Implement the lighting purchasing plan that specifies an overall building average of 70 picograms (*not* 20 picograms) of mercury per lumen-hour or less for all mercury-containing lamps purchased for the building and associated grounds within the project boundary.

Lamps containing no mercury may *not* always be counted. They may be counted *only if* their energy efficiency at least equals that of their mercury-containing counterparts.

107. Answer: a and c
The following are resources for Level 1 walk-through assessment:
- *2007 ASHRAE Handbook*
- *ASHRAE Procedures for Commercial Building Audits.*

See LEED O+M reference guide, EA Prerequisite: Energy Efficiency Best Management Practices.

108. Answer: e
See MR Credit: Purchasing—Lamps, under Performance section.

109. Answer: b and c
Please note we are looking for incorrect statements.

See MR Credit: Purchasing—Lamps.

LEED for Existing Buildings: Operation and Maintenance (LEED EB: OM) addresses only the lamps purchased during the performance period, not the lamps installed in the building.

LEED EB: OM requires only the overall average of purchased lamps must comply.

110. Answer: d
See SS Credit: Light Pollution Reduction,

111. Answer: c
See EA Credit: Optimize Energy Performance. For buildings eligible to receive an energy performance rating using the EPA ENERGY STAR's Portfolio Manager tool, points are awarded for ENERGY STAR scores above 75.

112. Answer: d
The maximum number of points that a project team can earn under EA Credit: Optimize Energy Performance is 20. See EA Credit: Optimize Energy Performance.

113. Answer: b and c
It takes energy to generate clean water and to maintain good indoor air quality. That is why EA Prerequisite: Energy Efficiency Best Management Practices is related to the following:
- WE Credit: Indoor Water Use Reduction
- EQ Credit: Indoor Air Quality Management Program

114. Answer: a
Factories are not eligible for Energy Star Ratings.

115. Answer: a
Regarding outdoor air monitoring for mechanically ventilated spaces under EQ Credit: Enhanced Indoor Air Quality Strategies, a

design team needs to provide a device capable of measuring the minimum outdoor airflow rate with an accuracy of within ± 10% of the design minimum outdoor air rate.

See section Outdoor Air Monitoring for Mechanically Ventilated Spaces: Establishment under EQ Credit: Enhanced Indoor Air Quality Strategies

116. Answer: c
For a multifamily project seeking LEED EB:O&M certification, a project team needs to maintain a waste reduction and recycling program that reuses, recycles, or composts at least 50% of the durable goods waste as specified in the Materials and Resources Prerequisite: Ongoing Purchasing and Waste Policy (by weight, volume, or replacement value).

Please note this is for a multifamily project.

See Performance section under Materials and Resources Prerequisite: Ongoing Purchasing and Waste Policy (by weight, volume, or replacement value).

117. Answer: e
Manual metering reading is not acceptable.
See EA Credit: Advanced Energy Metering.

118. Answer: a
General-purpose, bathroom, glass and carpet cleaners used for industrial and institutional

purposes shall be certified by the "Green Label" testing program.

See EQ Credit: Green Cleaning—Products and Materials.

"Green-e" testing program is for clean energy certification.

See link:
https://www.green-e.org/

The "Seal of Approval program" testing program is developed by the Carpet and Rug Institute to test and measure the effectiveness of cleaning products and equipment.

See link:
http://www.carpet-rug.org/seal-of-approval-program.html

EPA is the United States Environmental Protection Agency.

See link:
https://www.epa.gov/

119. Answer: d
For a school project seeking LEED EB:O&M certification, with regard to WE Credit: Indoor Water Use Reduction, a project team can earn 5 points if the indoor potable water use is reduced by 30%.

See WE Credit: Indoor Water Use Reduction, Table 1.

Chapter Two • 115

120. Answer: b
See EA Credit: Existing Building Commissioning—Implementation. The project team needs to create a capital plan for major upgrades or retrofits, but they do not need to implement *all* upgrades or retrofit for energy-using systems.

121. Answer: b and d
Please note we are looking for the following incorrect statements:
- Only work completed within one year prior to application may be included to show progress in the ongoing commissioning cycle.
- Ongoing commissioning is generally undertaken simultaneously with full retro-commissioning.

See EA Credit: Ongoing Commissioning

122. Answer: b and c
See EQ Credit: Enhanced Indoor Air Quality Strategies.

Each ventilation system that supplies outdoor air to occupied spaces must have particle filters or air cleaning devices. These filters or devices must meet *one of* the following filtration media requirements:
- minimum efficiency reporting value (MERV) of 13 or higher, in accordance with ASHRAE Standard 52.2–2007; (This is one of the two options, not the *only* mandatory requirement).

- Class F7 or higher as defined by CEN Standard EN 779–2002, Particulate Air Filters for General Ventilation, Determination of the Filtration Performance.

The correct answers to the question are:
- Establish a regular schedule for maintenance and replacement of filtration media according to the manufacturer's recommended interval.
- CO2 monitors must be between 3 and 6 feet above the floor.

123. Answer: b and e

See requirements of Carbon Dioxide Monitors of EQ Credit: Enhanced Indoor Air Quality Strategies.

CO2 monitors are required in all densely occupied spaces, rooms smaller than 150 sf are exempt.

A Janitor's room is not a densely occupied space.

124. Answer: a

Wood products designated as FSC Recycled are recycled content.

Recycled content refers to the portion of materials used in a product that have been diverted from the solid waste stream.

Recycled materials refer to materials that have been recycled.

Diverted materials refers to materials that have

been diverted from waste stream.

FSC-certified wood: Forest Stewardship Council (FSC) certification is an indicator, here in the U.S., that the wood was harvested sustainably.

125. Answer: c
 APPA refers to Association of Higher Education Facilities Officers.

 See link: www.appa.org

 The APPA's Custodial Staffing Guidelines include 5 levels of cleanliness:
 Level 1 - Orderly Spotlessness
 Level 2 - Ordinary Tidiness
 Level 3 - Casual Inattention
 Level 4 - Moderate Dinginess
 Level 5 - Unkempt Neglect

 Level 1 establishes cleaning at the highest level. Level 5 is the final and lowest level.

 The APPA's Custodial Staffing Guidelines is available at the following link:
 https://www.appa.org/files/general/allcustodialanalysis.pdf

 See EQ Credit: Green Cleaning—Custodial Effectiveness Assessment

126. Answer: a
 For a multitenant building, a project seeking LEED EB:O&M certification must involve a

minimum of 90% of the total gross floor area.

According to *LEED O+M reference guide*:
"Multitenant Buildings
Because certification applies to whole buildings, it may be challenging for multitenant buildings to earn certain credits, especially in the MR category. All portions of a building under the site management's control are expected to comply with the credit requirements. If it is not possible to gather to necessary information on purchasing or waste management to document credit achievement, or if the LEED applicant does not have control over the entire building, the project team may exempt up to 10% of the building's gross floor area."

127. Answer: a and d
Please pay attention to the word "except."
Colors and lamp types do *not* affect the targeted level of weighted average mercury content in lamps, and are therefore the correct answers.

128. Answer: a
For LEED EB:O&M, the baseline water use is determined by the year of substantial completion.

Section A.9.8.1 of the American Institute of Architects (AIA) document A201, General Conditions of the Contract for Construction, defines substantial completion as: "the stage in the progress of the Work when the Work or designated portion thereof is sufficiently complete in accordance with the Contract Documents so that the Owner can occupy or utilize the Work for its intended use."

129. Answer: c
Please pay attention to the word "except."

Surface waters are lakes and rivers, etc., and they should *not* be included when calculating stormwater runoff volumes using the rational method.

130. Answer: a
With regard to MR Prerequisite: Facility Maintenance and Renovation Policy, the minimum MERV for the filtration media that a project uses for inside air recirculation and outside air intake is 8.

See Section entitled: "Indoor Air Quality Policy for Maintenance and Renovations" Under MR Prerequisite: Facility Maintenance and Renovation Policy:
"Do not operate permanently-installed air handling equipment during construction unless filtration media with a minimum efficiency reporting value (MERV) of 8, as determined by ASHRAE 52.2–2007, with errata (or equivalent filtration media class of F5 or higher, as defined by CEN Standard EN 779–2002, Particulate Air Filters for General Ventilation, Determination of the Filtration Performance), are installed at each return air grille and return or transfer duct inlet opening such that there is no bypass around the filtration media."

131. Answer: b
Condensation is not related to chemical management of the cooling tower.

See Requirements under WE Credit: Cooling Tower Water Use.

Cooling tower **bleed-off/blowdown** is the flushing of a portion of high mineral concentration cooling tower system water down the drain, while simultaneously replacing it with fresh water.

Biological control is an important part of chemical management of the cooling tower.

Staff management can assure enough man power is assigned for chemical management of the cooling tower.

132. Answer: e
Answer "b" has some truth, but "e" is the best answer.

EPA's I-BEAM refers to the EPA Indoor Air Quality Building Education and Assessment Model. See the following link:
https://www.epa.gov/indoor-air-quality-iaq/indoor-air-quality-building-education-and-assessment-model

According to EQ Credit: Indoor Air Quality Management Program:
"**Establishment**
Develop and implement an indoor air quality (IAQ) management program based on the EPA Indoor Air Quality Building Education and Assessment Model (I-BEAM). Include the IAQ management program in the project's current

facilities requirements and operations and maintenance plan."

133. Answer: a
The environmental attributes of an on-site solar energy system need to be retained on-site, instead of by the power company, to earn LEED EB:O&M credits.

134. Answer: d
Visible light transmittance is related to daylighting.

See EQ Credit: Daylight and Quality Views.

Albedo is a measure for reflectance or optical brightness (Latin albedo, Arabic albayad, "whiteness"). It is dimensionless and measured on a scale from zero (corresponding to a black body that absorbs all incident radiation) to one (corresponding to a white body that reflects all incident radiation).

SRI refers to the solar reflectance index. It is a measure of the constructed surface's ability to reflect solar heat, as shown by a small temperature rise. It is defined so that a standard black surface (reflectance 0.05, emittance 0.90) is 0 and a standard white surface (reflectance 0.80, emittance 0.90) is 100.

Light pollution, also known as **photopollution**, is excessive, misdirected or obtrusive artificial light.

Daylighting is the illumination of buildings by natural light.

135. Answer: c
Recycling extra gypsum boards is not source reduction. The correct way of source reduction is ordering the correct quantity and grade of gypsum boards to begin with.

136. Answer: d
With regard to EQ Credit: Enhanced Indoor Air Quality Strategies, the length of the building entrance grate system should be 10 feet placed at the interior of the building.

137. Answer: d
SS Credit: Site Management addresses diversion from landfills 100% (*not* 80%) of plant material waste via low-impact means.

138. Answer: b
With regard to MR Credit: Purchasing—Ongoing, by cost, 60% of total ongoing consumables must meet at least one of the criteria listed in the performance section of the credit.

139. Answer: a and c
The following are true regarding
EQ Credit: Occupant Comfort Survey:
- Administer at least one occupant comfort survey.
- The responses must be collected from a representative sample of building occupants making up at least 30% of the total occupants.

140. Answer: b
Bleed-off is the process of draining a portion of the re-circulating water from the cooling tower.

141. Answer: a, d, and e
The advantages of chemical treatment in cooling towers are
- Reduction of potable water use
- Control of mineral deposits
- Prevention of legionella pneumophila outbreaks

142. Answer: b
With regard to WE Credit: Outdoor Water Use Reduction, a project team needs to demonstrate 40% of a reduction in outdoor water use over the most recent 12 months compared with the established baseline to achieve 2 points under Performance, Option 3.

143. Answer: a
Points can be earned for WE Credit: Indoor Water Use Reduction for having fixtures that use less water than the baseline calculated in WE Prerequisite Indoor Water-Use Reduction.

Installing sub-metering for at least 60% or 70% of the building area is not required and will not help the project team achieve points.

Using ANSI irrigation performance and ranking tools to show compliance is not required and will not help the project team achieve points.

144. Answer: e
The correct answer is "None of the above."

Pay attention to the word "not" in the question.

All of the following answers are related to WE Credit: Water Metering, and are therefore not the correct answer:
- Metering
- Sub-metering
- Process water
- Irrigation

145. Answer: c
The WE credit category is related to ENERGY STAR products.

Pay attention to the difference between ENERGY STAR products and ENERGY STAR rating; ENERGY STAR products are related to WE, but ENERGY STAR rating is related to EA.

146. Answer: b and c
See SS Credit: Light Pollution Reduction.

The following can help earn SS Credit: Light Pollution Reduction:
- Partially shield *all* (not 60%) exterior light fixtures to prevent emitting light into the night sky.
- Measure the night illumination levels at regularly spaced points on the project boundary.

All exterior light fixtures should be shielded such that the installed fixtures do not directly emit any light at a vertical angle more than 90 degrees from straight down.

Installing a monitoring system is not part of this credit requirements.

147. Answer: b and c
Please pay attention to the word "not,"

The following are not required to earn EA Credit: Ongoing Commissioning:
- Complete 100% of the scope of the work before submitting the application for LEED EB:O&M.
- Use only actual costs to document completed tasks.

See EA Credit: Ongoing Commissioning.

148. Answer: b and d
The following are not related to Building Automation System (BAS):
- Occupancy sensors
- Time clock

The following are part of BAS:
- DDC refers to the direct digital control. A smaller building may have a single, computerized HVAC controller that operates the direct digital control (DDC) system.
- Controlled devices
- Setpoints and setbacks

149. Answer: a
See MR Prerequisite: Ongoing Purchasing and Waste Policy. An Environmentally Preferable Purchasing (EPP) Policy is a mandatory prerequisite and cannot earn any point(s).

150. Answer: a
In an office building where the tenant turn-over rate is high, a furniture salvage program is the best sustainable strategy.

The following are good sustainable strategies, but not the best choices:
- Selling used furniture to recycled facilities
- Buying only furniture with pre- and postconsumer content

RECs refer to renewable energy certificates.

Green Seal is a non-profit environmental standard development and certification organization.

151. Answer: a
All typical HVAC equipment is assumed to have a life of 10 years.

See EA Credit: Enhanced Refrigerant Management.

152. Answer: d
See IN Credit: Innovation. A project team can achieve 1 to 5 points for this credit category.

153. Answer: b, c, and e
Pay attention to the word "except."

A project team must document the following in writing for Option 1. Innovation under IN Credit: Innovation:
- intent
- performance metric

The following are not required in the documentation, and therefore are the correct answers:
- definition
- strategies
- reference codes

See IN Credit: Innovation.

154. Answer: a, b, and d
With regard to EA Credit: Existing Building Commissioning—Implementation, the following changes will affect building operating plan updates:
- Lighting level
- Equipment run-time schedule
- Occupancy schedule

The following changes will *not* affect building operating plan updates:
- Sustainable purchase
- Solid waste management

155. Answer: a
Pay attention to the word "can."

If a project is certified under LEED EB:O&M, the project can be recertified every five years.

According to *LEED O+M Reference Guide*:
A LEED EB:O&M project <u>must</u> be recertified every five years to maintain certification, but <u>can</u> be recertified every year.

156. Answer: b
The maximum "gap" within a performance period is one week.

According to *LEED O+M Reference Guide*:
"LEED for Building Operations and Maintenance certification is based largely on successful outcomes during the performance period, when sustainable operations are being measured. Many prerequisites and credits require that operating data and other documentation be submitted for the performance period. Since the project's certification level is based on these outcomes, the performance period may *not* have any gaps, defined as any period of time longer than one full week."

157. Answer: a
According to EQ Credit: Occupant Comfort Survey:
"Administer at least one occupant comfort survey to collect anonymous responses regarding at least the following:
- acoustics;
- building cleanliness;

- indoor air quality;
- lighting; and
- thermal comfort.

The responses must be collected from a representative sample of building occupants making up at least 30% of the total occupants."

158. Answer: b and c
Please pay attention to the word "not."

The following are not a type of structural control for controlling erosion and sedimentation, and therefore the correct answers:
- Mulching
- Catch basin

The following are a type of structural control for controlling erosion and sedimentation:
- Silt fencing
- Earth dike

159. Answer: c and d
The following are not types of non-potable water that can be used for WE Credit: Cooling Tower Water Use, and therefore the correct answers:
- Naturally occurring groundwater
- Surface water

The following are types of non-potable water that can be used for WE Credit: Cooling Tower Water Use:
- Swimming pool filter backwash water
- Recycled treated wastewater from toilet and urinal flushing

160. Answer: a
An operations and maintenance plan is also called owner's operating requirements.

See EA Prerequisite: Energy Efficiency Best Management Practices.

161. Answer: b and d
With regard to a cooling tower, the following can help to prevent exposure to Legionella pneumophila:
- Biocides
- Well-maintained drift eliminators

The following cannot help to prevent exposure to Legionella pneumophila:
- The use of non-potable water
- Reducing evaporation
- The use of potable water

See WE Credit: Cooling Tower Water Use.

162. Answer: d
With regard to EA Credit: Optimize Energy Performance, for buildings eligible to receive an energy performance rating using the EPA ENERGY STAR's Portfolio Manager tool, points are awarded for ENERGY STAR scores above 75.

163. Answer: b
The minimum initial performance period for LEED EB:O&M is 3 months.

According to *LEED O+M Reference Guide*:
"The initial performance period is the most

recent period of operations preceding the certification application. It must be at least three months but no more than 24 months, except as noted in the credit requirements."

164. Answer: c
The maximum initial performance period for LEED EB:O&M is 24 months.

See *LEED O+M reference guide*.

165. Answer: d
For stormwater quantity control, a project team needs to perform all necessary stabilization, repairs, or routine required maintenance within 60 days of inspection.

According to SS Credit: Rainwater Management:

"PERFORMANCE
Document the annual inspections, including identification of areas of erosion, maintenance needs, and repairs. Perform necessary maintenance, repairs, or stabilization within 60 days of inspection."

166. Answer: d. None of the above
According to EQ Credit: Enhanced Indoor Air Quality Strategies:
"Outdoor Air Monitoring for Naturally Ventilated Spaces

Establishment
Provide a direct exhaust airflow measurement device capable of measuring the exhaust airflow.

This device must measure the exhaust airflow with an accuracy of +/–10% of the design minimum exhaust airflow rate. An alarm must indicate when airflow values vary by 15% or more from the exhaust airflow setpoint.

Performance
Calibrate all measurement devices within the manufacturer's recommended interval."

167. Answer: b and c
    The following are true with regard to EA Prerequisite: Energy Efficiency Best Management Practices:
    - The project team does not have to redo the walk-through analysis again.
    - The project team has to do an updated report.

168. Answer: a and b
    The following belong to operational effective credits:
    - Metering of energy use
    - Non-potable water use

169. Answer: a
    A $100 purchase that contains 60%, by cost, of total ongoing consumables that are postconsumer recycled content can be counted as $100 of sustainable purchasing.

    See MR Credit: Purchasing—Ongoing.

170. Answer: a and c
    A multifamily project seeking LEED EB:O&M certification can meet EQ Prerequisite: Minimum Indoor Air Quality Performance by

one of the two methods below:
- Meet ASHRAE 62.1-2010
- International projects may instead meet the alternative minimum outdoor air requirements.

171. Answer: b and d
    Please pay attention to the word "not."
    The following are not the I-BEAM protocols for managing major sources of pollution in buildings, and therefore the correct answers:
    - Using filters with proper MERV
    - Entry grates with sufficient length

    The following are the I-BEAM protocols for managing major sources of pollution in buildings:
    - Pest control
    - Shipping and receiving
    - Painting
    - Remodeling and renovation

172. Answer: b and d
    The following are strategies for promoting hand hygiene and compliance with green cleaning policy:
    - Use hand soaps without antimicrobial agents if allowed by codes.
    - Use waterless hand sanitizers.

173. Answer: b
    The non-respondents are considered as solo drivers, and the project cannot extrapolate the commuting behavior of the respondents to non-

respondents unless the response rate is 80% or more of the regular building occupants.

174. Answer: b

    With regard to EA Credit: Advanced Energy Metering, the project team must report the facility's utility peak demand and total consumption monthly.

    According to EA Credit: Advanced Energy Metering:
    "On at least a monthly basis, report the facility's utility peak demand and total consumption and compare it with the data for the previous month and the same month from the previous year."

175. Answer: c

    With regard to light pollution reduction, if the top of a window glass is 8 feet from the floor, the exempt distance from the window for an interior light that is above the top of the window glass is 12 feet.

176. Answer: a and d

    With regard to the building exterior and hardscape management plan, the following are less environmentally friendly ways of snow and ice removal:
    - Calcium chloride
    - Sodium chloride

    According to SS Credit: Site Management:
    "Use no calcium chloride or sodium chloride deicers, and/or establish reduced treatment areas equal to 50% of applicable paving area."

This is because calcium chloride and sodium chloride deicers are harmful.

177. Answer: a
The energy-use intensity should be calculated as Total kBtu/Gross Floor Area

Also see EA Prerequisite: Energy Efficiency Best Management Practices.

178. Answer: a
The intent of ASHRAE Level walk-through is to conduct an energy audit.

179. Answer: a
If a project is not eligible for an Energy Star Rating, it must be 25% more energy efficient than the average of similar types of buildings in the nation to qualify for LEED EB:O&M certification.

According to EA Prerequisite: Minimum Energy Performance:
"Case 2. Projects Not Eligible for ENERGY STAR Rating
Projects not eligible to use EPA's rating system may compare their buildings' energy performance with that of comparable buildings, using national averages or actual buildings, or with the previous performance of the project building.
Option 1. Benchmark against Typical Buildings
Path 1. National Average Data Available
Demonstrate energy efficiency performance that is 25% better than the median energy

performance of similar buildings by benchmarking against the national source energy data provided in the Portfolio Manager tool."

180. Answer: d
Systems narrative lists each distinct type of system, such as humidification, dehumidification, ventilation, space cooling, etc. See EA Prerequisite: Energy Efficiency Best Management Practices.

181. Answer: b, e, and f
The following are ineligible on-site renewable systems:
- Passive solar strategies
- Daylighting strategies
- Geoexchange systems

182. Answer: b
A project seeking LEED EB:O&M certification can earn a maximum of 2 points for exemplary performance under IN Credit: Innovation:
"Exemplary Performance (1–2 points)
Achieve exemplary performance in an existing LEED v4 prerequisite or credit that allows exemplary performance, as specified in the LEED Reference Guide, v4 edition. An exemplary performance point is typically earned for achieving double the credit requirements or the next incremental percentage threshold."

183. Answer: b
A project seeking LEED EB:O&M certification can earn a maximum of 4 points for RP Credit: Regional Priority.

184. Answer: d
 According to Credit: Site Development—Protect or Restore Habitat:
 **"Option 1. On-Site Restoration (2 points)
 Establishment**
 Have in place native or adapted vegetation on 20% of the total site area (including the building footprint), a minimum of 5,000 square feet (465 square meters), to provide habitat and promote biodiversity."

 The building footprint (10,000 sf) is a distracter. This question also tests your basic and common construction knowledge:
 1 acre = 43,560 sf
 20% of the site area = 20% x 43,560 sf = 8,712 sf

185. Answer: d
 CIBSE refers to the Chartered Institution of Building Services Engineers.

 The CIBSE Application Manual is related to Ventilation.

 According to EQ Prerequisite: Minimum Indoor Air Quality Performance:
 "Naturally Ventilated Spaces
 For naturally ventilated spaces (and for mixed-mode systems when the mechanical ventilation is inactivated), determine the minimum outdoor air opening and space configuration requirements using the natural ventilation procedure from ASHRAE Standard 62.1–2010 or a local equivalent, whichever is more

stringent. Confirm that natural ventilation is an effective strategy for the project by following the flow diagram in the Chartered Institution of Building Services Engineers (CIBSE) Applications Manual AM10, March 2005, Natural Ventilation in Nondomestic Buildings, Figure 2.8 and meet the requirements of ASHRAE Standard 62.1–2010, Section 4, or a local equivalent, whichever is more stringent."

186. Answer: b, d, and e

A detailed plan for ongoing commissioning must include:
- Measurement requirements
- Review process
- Frequency of analyses

EA Credit: Ongoing Commissioning requires a project team to:
"Develop an on-going commissioning plan that defines the following:
- roles and responsibilities;
- measurement requirements (meters, points, metering systems, data access);
- the points to be tracked, with frequency and duration for trend monitoring;
- the limits of acceptable values for tracked points and metered values;
- the review process that will be used to evaluate performance;
- an action plan for identifying and correcting operational errors and deficiencies;
- planning for repairs needed to maintain performance;
- the frequency of analyses in the first year (at

least quarterly); and
- the subsequent analysis cycle (at least every 24 months)."

187. Answer: b and c
    The following are true:
    - A project must have an Energy Star Rating of 75 or higher to earn an Energy Star Label.
    - A project that is not eligible for an Energy Star Label can earn LEED certification.

    According to EA Credit: Optimize Energy Performance:
    "**Case 1. ENERGY STAR Rating (3–20 points)**
    For buildings eligible to receive an energy performance rating using the EPA ENERGY STAR's Portfolio Manager tool, points are awarded for ENERGY STAR scores above 75…

    Case 2. Projects Not Eligible for ENERGY STAR Rating
    Projects not eligible to use EPA's rating system may compare their buildings' energy performance with that of comparable buildings, using national averages or actual buildings, or with the previous performance of the project building."

188. Answer: b
    In an unincorporated area with no codes regarding erosion control, a project team follows EPA's Stormwater Pollution Prevention Plans.

    CPESC refers to Certified Professional in Erosion and Sediment Control. It is a qualification indicating the holder has educational training, expertise and experience in controlling erosion and sedimentation, and met certification standards.

IPM refers to Integrated Pest Management. It is an environmentally friendly, common sense approach to controlling pests.

Erosion Control Technical Council
is an invented term used as a distractor. A similar term is Erosion Control Technology Council (ECTC).

189. Answer: c
With regard to LT Credit: Alternative Transportation, Alternative Commuting Transportation includes all listed items except expanded workweeks.

Expanded workweeks will increase the number of workdays and work-related trips, and will generate more traffic. *Compressed* workweeks will alleviate traffic problems.

190. Answer: c
A vegetated roof can contribute to all but EQ Credit: Daylight and Quality Views.

191. Answer: c
EA Credit: Existing Building Commissioning—Analysis is related to ASHRAE Level 2 Energy Audit.

According to EA Credit: Existing Building Commissioning—Analysis:

"Option 2. Energy Audit
Develop an energy audit plan following the requirements of ASHRAE Level 2, Energy Survey and Analysis, to evaluate efficiency opportunities."

The main difference between ASHRAE Audit Level 1, 2, and 3 are as follows:

"ASHRAE Audit Level 1 – Walk-Through Analysis: This energy audit involves interviews with select facility staff, a review of utility bills or other operating data and a walk through of the facility…

ASHRAE Audit Level 2 – Energy Survey and Analysis: This includes the ASHRAE Level 1 analysis, but adds detailed energy calculations and financial analysis of proposed energy efficiency measures…

ASHRAE Audit Level 3 – Detailed Analysis of Capital Intensive Modifications: This focuses on an engineering analysis of the potential capital-intensive projects identified in the ASHRAE Level 2 Analysis…"

For detailed info, see the following link:
https://www.smartwatt.com/whats-difference-ashrae-level-1-2-3-audits/

192. Answer: a
See EA Credit: Existing Building Commissioning—Analysis. This follows the latest ASHRAE Handbook, NOT the 1996

ASHRAE Handbook.

193. Answer: c

Excluding skylights, photovoltaic panels, and mechanical equipment, the following will help a project earn an IN Credit: Innovation Exemplary Performance point:

- (Area of Roof Meeting Minimum SRI/Total Roof Area) x (SRI of Installed Roof/Required SRI) ≥ 75%

See Exemplary Performance under SS Credit: Heat Island Reduction

194. Answer: e. None of the above.

LEED v4 does not have SS Credit: LEED Certified Design and Construction. This is a trick question to confuse you. If you firmly understand and master the LEED O&M system, you will do fine in the real exam.

195. Answer: c

Per Energy Star Rating System, an average building's performance is 50.

According to Energy Star's official website (EnergyStar.gov):

"What your 1 – 100 ENERGY STAR score means?

The 1 – 100 ENERGY STAR score is a screening tool that helps you assess how your building is performing. It'll help you identify which buildings in your portfolio to target for improvement or recognition. A score of 50 is the median. So if your building scores below 50, it means it's performing worse than 50 percent of similar buildings nationwide, while a score above 50 means it's performing better than 50 percent of its peers. And a score of 75 or higher means it's a top performer and may be eligible for ENERGY STAR certification."

196. Answer: a
With regard to the EA Credit: Ongoing Commissioning, only work completed within two years prior to application may be included to show progress in the ongoing commissioning cycle.

According to EA Credit: Ongoing Commissioning:
"Only activities associated with ongoing commissioning completed within two years of the LEED application may be included to show progress."

197. Answer: c
With regard to SS Credit: Light Pollution Reduction, shielding exterior fixtures to prevent them from emitting any light at certain angle can help a project to earn one point.

According to SS Credit: Light Pollution Reduction:
"Option 1. Fixture Shielding
Shield all exterior fixtures (where the sum of the mean lamp lumens for that fixture exceeds 2,500) such that the installed fixtures do not directly emit any light at a vertical angle more than 90 degrees from straight down."

198. Answer: a
With regard to MR Credit: Purchasing—Facility Maintenance and Renovation, exterior sealant must comply with SCAQMD.

According to MR Credit: Purchasing—Facility Maintenance and Renovation:
"All adhesives and sealants wet-applied on site must meet the applicable chemical content requirements of SCAQMD Rule 1168, July 1, 2005, Adhesive and Sealant Applications, as analyzed by the methods specified in Rule 1168. The provisions of SCAQMD Rule 1168 do not apply to adhesives and sealants subject to state or federal consumer product VOC regulations."

Green Seal's Standard GS-11, Environmental Choice CCD-110, or SMACNA is not referred to in this credit.

SMACNA refers to the Sheet Metal and Air Conditioning National Contractors Association.

199. Answer: a and c
A project team is seeking an Energy Star Rating for a building, EPA allows the exclusion of up to 10% of gross floor area if:
- the space does not fit any of the Energy Star space type classifications.
- the energy use of that space is submetered.

See EA Credit: Optimize Energy Performance for related information.

200. Answer: b

A project team can use eGRID Subregions to relate the emissions from a building's energy consumption to the source of that energy.

NERC refers to North American Electric Reliability Corporation. It was formed on June 1, 1968, by the electric utility industry to promote the reliability and adequacy of bulk power transmission in the electric utility systems of North America.

Portfolio Manager refers to the Environmental Protection Agency (EPA) ENERGY STAR Portfolio Manager tool.

201. Answer: d

SS Credit: Light Pollution Reduction cannot earn exemplary performance points.

See *LEED O+M Reference Guide*, page 22, Getting Start, Quick Reference, Table 3, Credit Attributes. Each credit that can or cannot earn exemplary performance is listed in the table.

LEED AP O+M Exam only has 200 questions in total. This question 201 is an extra question, and a free gift from me.

III. How were the LEED AP O+M mock exams created?

The actual LEED AP O+M Exam has 200 questions (100 questions for each section) and you must finish it within four hours. The raw exam score is converted to a scaled score ranging from 125 to 200. The passing score is 170 or higher.

I tried to be scientific when selecting the mock exam questions, so I based the number of questions for each credit category roughly on the number of points that you can get for that category. The level of difficulty for each question was designed to match the official sample questions that can be downloaded from the official GBCI website. Feedback from our readers has indicated that this mock exam is relatively easy when compared to the actual LEED AP O+M Exam.

IV. Where can I find the latest and official sample questions for the LEED AP O+M Exam?

Answer: You can find them, as well as the exam content, from the candidate handbook, at: http://www.usgbc.org/resources/leed-v4-ap-om-candidate-handbook

V. Latest trend for LEED exams

Recently, there are quite a few readers run into the versions of the LEED exams that have many questions on refrigerants (CFC, HCFC, and HFC), the following advice will help you answer these questions correctly:

For more information, see free pdf file of "The Treatment by LEED of the Environmental Impact of HVAC Refrigerants" that you can download at link below:

http://www.usgbc.org/resources/treatment-leed-environmental-impact-hvac-refrigerants

This is a VERY important document that you need to become familiar with. Many real LEED exam questions (CFC, HCFC, and HFC, etc.) come from this document. You need to download it for free and read it at least 3 times.

Pay special attention to the Table on ODP and GWP on page 3. You do not have to remember the exact value of all ODPs and GWPs, but you do need to know the rough number for various groups of refrigerants."

This latest trend regarding refrigerants (CFC, HCFC, and HFC) for LEED Exams has a lot to do with LEED v4 Credit Weighting. EA (including refrigerants) is a big winner in LEED v4, meaning the category has MORE questions than any other areas for ALL the LEED exams. See portion of my book, *LEED GA Exam Guide* quoted below:

How are LEED credits allocated and weighted?
Answer: Credits that can contribute to LEED's **"Impact Categories"** are given more points. These impact categories are weighted through a consensus driven process and are as follows:
- global **climate change** (35%)
- social equity, environmental justice, and **community** quality of life (5%)
- individual **human health** and well-being (20%)
- **greener economy** (5%)
- **biodiversity** and Ecosystem (10%)
- **water resources** (15%)
- sustainable and regenerative **material resources** cycles (10%)

The USGBC uses three **association factors** to measure and scale credit outcome to a given impact category component.
1) **Relative efficacy** measures whether a credit outcome has a positive or negative association with a given Impact Category component, and how strong that association is. They're rated as follows:
    - no association
    - low association
    - medium association
    - high association
    - negative association

2) **Benefit duration** measures how long the benefits or consequences of the credit outcome will last:
    - 1-3 Years
    - 4-10 Years
    - 11-30 Years

- 30+ Years (Building/Community Lifetime)

3) **Controllability of effect** indicates which individual is most directly responsible for achieving the expected credit outcome. The more a credit outcome depends on active human effort, the less likely it will be achieved with certainty, and the credit will have fewer points. Less human effort equals more points.

The USGBC simplifies the weighting process of points into a **scorecard computed as follows**:
- **100 base points** for the base LEED Rating System
- **1 point minimum** for each credit
- **whole points** and no fractions for LEED points

See detailed discussions in the FREE PDF file entitled "LEED v4 Impact Category and Point Allocation Development Process" at the following link:
http://www.usgbc.org/sites/default/files/LEED%20v4%20Impact%20Category%20and%20Point%20Allocation%20Process_Overview_0.pdf

VI. LEED AP O+M Exam registration

1. **How to register for the LEED AP O+M Exam?**
   Answer: In the latest candidate handbook, you will find detailed instructions on how to register for an LEED exam and set up an exam time and date with Prometric. You can reschedule or cancel the LEED AP O+M Exam at www.prometric.com/gbci with your Prometric-issued confirmation number for the exam. You

need to bring two forms of ID to the exam site. See www.prometric.com/gbci for a list of exam sites. Call 1-800-795-1747 (within the US) or 202-742-3792 (Outside of the US) or e-mail exam@gbci.org if you have any questions.

2. **Important Note:**
   You can download the "LEED AP O+M Candidate Handbook" from the USGBC website and get all the latest details and procedures. Ideally you should download it and read it carefully at least three weeks before your exam.

   Refer to the following links:
   http://www.usgbc.org/resources/leed-v4-ap-om-candidate-handbook

Chapter Three

Frequently Asked Questions (FAQ) and Other Useful Resources

The following are tips on how to pass the LEED exam on the first try with only one week of preparation. I also include my responses to several readers' questions. Hopefully they may help you.

I. **I found the reference guide way too tedious. Can I only read your books and just refer to the USGBC reference guide (if one is available for the exam I am taking) when needed?**

    Response: Yes. That is one way to study.

II. **Is one week really enough for me to prepare for the exam while I am working?**
    Response: Yes, if you can put in 40 to 60 hours during the week, study hard and you can pass the exam. This exam is similar to a history or political science exam; you need to MEMORIZE the information. If you take too long, you will

probably forget the information by the time you take the test.

In my book, I give you tips on how to MEMORIZE the information, and I have already highlighted/underlined the most important information that you definitely have to MEMORIZE to pass the exam. It is my goal to use this book to help you to pass the LEED exam with the minimum time and effort. I want to make your life easier.

III. **Would you say that if I buy your LEED Exam Guide Series books, I could pass the exam using no other study materials? The books sold on the USGBC website run in the hundreds of dollars, so I would be quite happy if I could buy your book and just use that.**

Response: First of all, there are readers who have passed the LEED Exam by reading only my books in the LEED Exam Guides series (www.GreenExamEducation.com). My goal is to write at least one book for each of the LEED exams, and my books stand alone to prepare people for one specific LEED exam.

Secondly, people learn in many different ways. That is why I have added some new advice below for people who learn better by doing practice tests.

If you do the following things, you have a very good chance of passing the LEED exam (NOT a guarantee, nobody can guarantee you will pass):

a. If you study, understand and MEMORIZE all of the information in my books, and do NOT panic when you run into problems you are not familiar with, and use the guess strategy in my books, then you have a very good chance of passing the exam.

You need to UNDERSTAND and MEMORIZE the information in the books and score almost a perfect score on the mock exam in my book. This book will give you the BULK of the most CURRENT information that you need for the specific LEED exam you are taking. You HAVE to know the information in my book in order to pass the exam.

b. If you have not done any LEED projects before, I suggest you also go to the USGBC website and download the latest LEED credit templates for the LEED rating system related to the LEED exam you are taking. Read the templates and become familiar with them. This is important. Refer to the following link: http://www.usgbc.org/leed#rating

The LEED exam is NOT an easy exam, but anyone with a 7th grade education should be able to study and pass the LEED exam if he prepares correctly.

If you have extra time and money, the other books I would recommend is *LEED GA Mock Exams (LEED v4)* and the USGBC reference guide, the official book for the LEED exam. I know some people who did not even read the reference guide from cover to cover when they took the exam. They just studied the information in my books, and only referred to the reference guide to look up a few things, and they passed on the first try. Some of my readers have even passed WITHOUT reading the USGBC reference guide AT ALL.

IV. I am preparing for the LEED exam. Do I need to read the 2" thick reference?

Response: See answer above.

V. For LEED v4, will the total number of points be more than 110 in total if a project gets all of the extra credits and all of the standard credits?

Response: No. For LEED v4, there are <u>100</u> base points and <u>10</u> possible bonus points. There are many ways to get bonus points (extra credits or exemplary performance), but you can have a maximum number of <u>6 ID</u> bonus points and <u>4 Regional Priority</u> bonus points. So, the maximum points for ANY project will be <u>110</u>.

On another note, the older versions of LEED rating systems all have less than 110 possible points except LEED for **Home**, which has 136 possible points.

VI. For the exam, do I need to know the project phase in which a specific prerequisite/credit takes place? (i.e., pre-design, schematic design, etc.)

Response: The information on the project phase (NOT LEED submittal phase) for each prerequisite/credit is NOT mentioned in the USGBC reference guide, but it is covered in the USGBC workshops. If it is important enough for the USGBC workshops to cover, then it may show up on the actual LEED exam.

Most, if not all, other third party books completely miss this important information. I cover it for each prerequisite/credit in my books for the LEED exam because I think it is very important.

Some people THINK that the LEED exam ONLY tests information covered by the USGBC reference guide. They are wrong.

The LEED exam does test information NOT covered by the USGBC reference guide at all. This may include the process of LEED submittal and project team coordination, etc.

I would MEMORIZE this information if I were you, because it may show up on the LEED exam. Besides, this information is not hard to memorize once you understand it, and you need to know it to do actual LEED submittal work anyway.

VII. **Are you writing new versions of books for the new LEED exams? What new books are you writing?**

Response: Yes, I am working on other books in the LEED Exam Guide series. I will be writing one book for each of the LEED exam. See GreenExamEducation.com for more information.

VIII. **Important documents that you need to download for <u>free</u>, become familiar with and <u>memorize</u>:**

Note: GBCI and USGBC change the links to their document every now and then, so, by the time you read this book, they may have changed some of the following links. You can simply go to their main website, search for the document with its name, and should be able to find the most current link. You can use the same technique to search for documents by other organizations.
The main website for the GBCI is:
http://www.gbci.org/
The main website for the USGBC is:
http://www.usgbc.org/

a. Every LEED exam **always tests** Credit Interpretation Request (CIR). Read and <u>memorize</u> the information at the following link: http://www.usgbc.org/help/what-project-credit-interpretation-ruling-cir

Every LEED exam **always tests** project team

coordination. Download *Sustainable Building Technical Manual: Part II,* by Anthony Bernheim and William Reed, read and memorize it:
http://www.usgbc.org/resources/sustainable-building-technical-manual-part-ii-predesign-issues

b. Project registration application and LEED certification process:
http://www.usgbc.org/LEED

c. LEED Online:
https://leedonline.usgbc.org/Login.aspx

IX. **Important documents that you need to download for free, and become familiar with:**

a. *LEED for Operations and Maintenance Reference Guide-Introduction* (U.S. Green Building Council, 2013):
http://www.usgbc.org/sites/all/assets/section/files/v4-guide-excerpts/Excerpt_v4_OM.pdf

b. Glossary: The terms below are applicable to LEEDv4: BD+C (except Homes and Multifamily Midrise), ID+C, and O+M:
http://www.usgbc.org/glossary/

c. *LEED for Homes Rating System* (U.S. Green Building Council): http://www.usgbc.org/cert-guide/homes

d. *Cost of Green Revisited,* by Davis Langdon (2007):

http://sustainability.ucr.edu/docs/leed-cost-of-green.pdf

e. *The Treatment by LEED® of the Environmental Impact of HVAC Refrigerants (*LEED Technical and Scientific Advisory Committee, 2004): http://www.usgbc.org/resources/treatment-leed-environmental-impact-hvac-refrigerants

f. *Guidance on Innovation and Design (ID) Credits* (US Green Building Council, 2004): http://www.usgbc.org/Docs/LEEDdocs/IDcredit_guidance_final.pdf

X. Do I need to take many practice questions to prepare for a LEED exam?

Response: There is NO absolutely correct answer to this question. People learn in many different ways. Personally, I am NOT crazy about doing many practice questions. Consider if you do 700 practice questions, not only must you read them all, but each question has at least 4 choices. That totals to at least 2,800 choices, which is a great deal of reading. I have seen some third-party materials that have 1,200 practice questions. That will require even MORE time to go over the materials.

I prefer to spend most of my time reading, digesting, and really understanding the fundamental materials, and MEMORIZE them naturally by rereading the materials multiple times. This is because the fundamental materials for ANY exam will NOT change, and the scope of the exam will NOT change for the same main version of the test (until the exam moves to the next advanced version). However, there are many ways to ask you questions.

If you have a limited amount of time for preparation, it is more efficient for you to focus on the fundamental materials and actually master the knowledge that GBCI wants you to learn. If you can do that, then no matter how GBCI changes the exam format or how GBCI asks the questions, you will do fine in the exam.

Strategy 101 for the LEED AP O+M Exam is that you must recognize that you have only a limited amount of time to prepare for the exam. Therefore, you must concentrate on the most important contents of the LEED AP O+M Exam.

The key to passing the LEED AP O+M Exam, or any other exam, is to know the scope of the exam, and not to read too many books. Select one or two helpful books and focus on them. You must understand the content and memorize it. For your convenience, I have underlined the fundamental information that I think is very important. You definitely need to memorize all the information that I have underlined. You should try to understand the content first, and then memorize the content of the book by rereading it multiple times. This is a much better way than "mechanical" memory without understanding.

Most people fail the exam NOT because they are unable to answer the few "advanced" questions on the exam, but because they have read the information but can NOT recall it on the day of the exam. They spend too much time preparing for the exam, drag the preparation process on too long, seek too much information, go to too many Web sites, do too many practice questions and too many mock exams (one or two sets of mock exams are probably sufficient), and spread themselves too thin. They end up missing out on the most important information of the LEED exam, and they will fail.

To me, Memorization and understanding work hand-in-hand. Understanding always comes first. If you really understand something, then Memorization is easy.

For example, I'll read a book's first chapter very slowly but make sure I <u>really</u> understand everything in it, no matter how long it takes. I do NOT care if others are faster readers than I. Then, I reread the first chapter again. This time, the reading is so much easier, and I can read it much faster. Then I try to retell the contents, focusing on substance, not the format or any particular order of things. This is a very good way for me to understand and digest the material, while <u>absorbing</u> and <u>memorizing</u> the content.

I then repeat the same procedure for each chapter, and then reread the book until I take the exam. This achieves two purposes:

a. I keep reinforcing the important materials that I already have memorized and fight against the human brain's natural tendency to forget things.

b. I also understand the content of the book much better by reading it multiple times.

If I were to attempt to memorize something without understanding it first, it would be very difficult for me to do so. Even if I were to memorize it, I would likely forget it quickly.

Appendixes

I. Default occupancy factors

Occupancy	Gross sf per occupant	
	Transient Occupant	FTE
Educational, Daycare	630	105
Educational, K–12	1,300	140
Educational, Postsecondary	2,100	150
Grocery store	550	115
Hotel	1,500	700
Laboratory or R&D	400	0
Office, Medical	225	330
Office, General	250	0
Retail, General	550	130
Retail or Service (auto, financial, etc.)	600	130
Restaurant	435	95
Warehouse, Distribution	2,500	0
Warehouse, Storage	20,000	0

Note: This table is for projects (like CS) where the final occupant count is not available. If your project's occupancy factors are not listed above, you can use a comparable building to show the average gross sf per occupant for your building's use.

II. Official reference materials listed by the GBCI

For Exam Part 1: LEED® Green Associate™ Exam:

U.S. Green Building Council. *Green Building and LEED Core Concepts Guide*. 3rd Edition. U.S. Green Building Council, 2011. Print and Digital versions available.
http://www.usgbc.org/resources/leed-core-concepts-guide

U.S. Green Building Council. *Introductory and Overview Sections. LEED Building Design + Construction Reference Guide*. v4 Edition. U.S. Green Building Council, 2013. *Note: the introductory and overview sections are available to download for FREE, separately from purchasing the full reference guide.*
http://www.usgbc.org/resources/leed-reference-guide-building-design-and-construction.

U.S. Green Building Council. *LEED v4 Impact Category and Point Allocation Process Overview*. U.S. Green Building Council, 2013.
http://www.usgbc.org/resources/leed-v4-

impact-category-and-point-allocation-process-overview

U.S. Green Building Council. *LEED v4 User Guide*. U.S. Green Building Council, 2013.
http://www.usgbc.org/resources/leed-v4-user-guide

U.S. Green Building Council. *Guide to LEED Certification: Commercia*l. U.S. Green Building Council, 2014.
http://www.usgbc.org/resources/guide-leed-certification-commerical

"LEED Certification Fees." U.S. Green Building Council, 2014.
http://www.usgbc.org/cert-guide/fees

"Rating System Selection Guidance." U.S. Green Building Council, 2014.
http://www.usgbc.org/resources/rating-system-selection-guidance

Exam Part 2: LEED AP O+M Specialty Exam

U.S. Green Building Council. *LEED Reference Guide for Building Operations and Maintenance*. v4 Edition. U.S. Green Building Council, 2013.
http://www.usgbc.org/resources/leed-reference-guide-building-operations-and-

maintenance

"Good to know: Green building incentive strategies." U. S. Green Building Council. http://www.usgbc.org/articles/good-know-green-building-incentive-strategies-0

U.S. Green Building Council. *Guide to LEED Certification: Commercial*. U.S. Green Building Council.
http://www.usgbc.org/cert-guide/commercial

U.S. Green Building Council. *Foundations of LEED*. U.S. Green Building Council, 2009.
http://www.usgbc.org/resources/foundations-leed

U.S. Green Building Council. *Checklist: LEED v4 for Building Operations and Maintenance*. U.S. Green Building Council.
http://www.usgbc.org/resources/checklist-leed-v4-building-operations-and-maintenance

"LEED Addenda Database (Corrections + Interpretations)." U. S. Green Building Council.
http://www.usgbc.org/resources/leed-addenda-database

LEED Online. U.S. Green Building Council.
https://lo.usgbc.org/

"LEED Certification Fees." U.S. Green Building Council.
http://www.usgbc.org/cert-guide/fees

"LEED v4 Rating System Selection Guidance." U.S. Green Building Council.
http://www.usgbc.org/articles/rating-system-selection-guidance

III. Important resources and further study materials you can download for <u>free</u>

Energy Performance of LEED® for New Construction Buildings: Final Report, by Cathy Turner and Mark Frankel (2008):
http://newbuildings.org/resource/energy-performance-leed-new-construction-buildings/

Foundations of the Leadership in Energy and Environmental Design Environmental Rating System: A Tool for Market Transformation (LEED Steering Committee, 2006):
http://www.usgbc.org/redirect.php?DocumentID=626

AIA Integrated Project Delivery: A Guide (www.aia.org):
https://www.aiacontracts.org/resources/64146-integrated-project-delivery-a-guide

Review of ANSI/ASHRAE Standard 62.1-2004: Ventilation for Acceptable Indoor Air Quality, by Brian Kareis:
http://www.workplace-hygiene.com/articles/ANSI-ASHRAE-3.html

Best Practices of ISO - 14021: Self-Declared Environmental Claims, by Kun-Mo Lee and Haruo Uehara (2003):
http://books.google.be/books/about/Best_practices_of_ISO_14021.html?hl=nl&id=e2eCAAAACAAJ

Bureau of Labor Statistics (www.bls.gov)

International Code Council (www.iccsafe.org)

Americans with Disabilities Act (ADA): Standards for Accessible Design (www.ada.gov):
http://www.ada.gov/stdspdf.htm

GSA Facilities Standards (General Services Administration, Latest Edition):
http://www.gsa.gov/portal/content/104821

Guide to Purchasing Green Power (Environmental Protection Agency, 2004):
https://www.epa.gov/greenpower/guide-purchasing-green-power

USGBC Definitions: https://www.usgbc.org/ShowFile.aspx?DocumentID=5744

IV. Annotated bibliography

Chen, Gang. *LEED v4 Green Associate Exam Guide (LEED GA): Comprehensive Study Materials, Sample Questions, Mock Exam, Green Building LEED Certification, and Sustainability*, Book 2, LEED Exam Guide series, ArchiteG.com. Latest Edition ArchiteG, Inc. This is a very comprehensive and concise book on the LEED Green Associate Exam. Some readers have passed the LEED Green Associate Exam by studying this book for 10 hours in total.

Chen, Gang. *LEED GA MOCK EXAMS (LEED v4): Questions, Answers, and Explanations: A Must-Have for the LEED Green Associate Exam, Green Building LEED Certification, and Sustainability*. Latest Edition. ArchiteG, Inc. This is a companion to **LEED Green Associate Exam Guide**. It includes 200 questions, answers, and explanation, and is very close to the real LEED Green Associate Exam.

Chen, Gang. *LEED v4 BD&C EXAM GUIDE: A Must-Have for the LEED AP BD+C Exam: Study Materials, Sample Questions, Green Building Design and*

Construction, LEED Certification, and Sustainability. LEED Exam Guide series, ArchiteG.com. Latest Edition ArchiteG, Inc. This is a very comprehensive and concise book on the LEED AP BD+C Exam. Some readers have passed the LEED Green Associate Exam by studying only these two books: ***LEED v4 BD&C EXAM GUIDE*** and ***LEED v4 BD&C Mock Exam***.

Chen, Gang. ***LEED v4 BD&C Mock Exam****: Questions, answers, and explanations: A must-have for the LEED AP BD+C Exam, green building LEED certification, and sustainability.* LEED Exam Guide series, ArchiteG.com. Latest Edition ArchiteG, Inc. This is a companion to ***LEED v4 BD&C EXAM GUIDE***. It includes 200 questions, answers, and explanation, and is very close to the real AP BD+C Exam.

V. Valuable Web sites and links

a. The Official Websites for the U.S. Green Building Council (USGBC):
http://www.usgbc.org/
http://www.Greenbuild365.org

Pay special attention to the purpose of <u>LEED Online, LEED project registration, LEED certification content, LEED reference guide introductions, LEED rating systems, and checklists</u>.

You can download or purchase the following useful documents from the USGBC or GBCI website:

Latest and official LEED exam candidate handbooks including an exam content outline and sample questions:
http://www.usgbc.org/resources/list/credentialing-resources

LEED Reference Guides:
http://www.usgbc.org/store/products/publications

LEED Rating System Selection:
http://www.usgbc.org/certification

Read the document above *at least three times*, because it is very important, and tells you which LEED system to use.

Various versions of LEED Green Building Rating Systems and Project Checklist:
http://www.usgbc.org/resources/grid/LEED

USGBC issue LEED Addenda for various LEED Green Building Rating **Systems** and **reference guides** on a quarterly basis. **Make sure you download the latest LEED Addenda** related to your exam and read them at least three times.

See link below for detailed information: http://www.usgbc.org/resources/leed-addenda-database

b. Natural Resources Defense Council: http://www.nrdc.org/

s. Cool Roof Rating Council website: http://www.coolroofs.org

VI. Important Items Covered by the Second Edition of *Green Building and LEED Core Concepts Guide*

Starting on December 1, 2011, GBCI will begin to draw LEED Green Associate Exam questions from the second edition of *Green Building and LEED Core Concepts Guide*. The following are some "new" and important items covered by this edition:

adaptive reuse: Designing and constructing a building to accommodate a future use that is different from its original use.

biomimicry: Learning from nature and designing systems using principles that have been tested in nature for millions of years.

carbon overlay: LEED credit weighting based on each credit's impact on reducing carbon footprint.

charrettes: Intensive (design) workshops.

cradle to cradle: A method where materials are used in a closed system and generate no waste.

cradle to grave: A process that examines materials from their point of extraction to disposal.

closed system: There is no "away." Everything goes somewhere within the system, the waste generated by a process becomes the "food" of another process. Nature is a closed system.

embodied energy: The total energy consumed by extracting, harvesting, manufacturing, transporting, installing, and using a material through its entire life cycle.

ENERGY STAR's Portfolio Manager: An online management tool for tracking and evaluating water and energy use. An ENERGY STAR Portfolio Manager score of 50 means a building is at national average energy use level for its category. A score higher than 50 means a building is more energy efficient than the national average energy use level for its category. The higher the score, the better.

evapotranspiration: Loss of water due to evaporation.

externalities: Benefits or costs that are NOT part of a transaction.

feedback loop: Information flows within a system that allows the system to adjust itself. A thermostat or melting snow is an example of negative feedback loop. Population growth, heat island effect, or climate change is a positive feedback loop. Positive feedback loop can create chaos in a system.

International Green Construction Code (IGCC): A national model green building code published by International Code Council (ICC).

integrated process: Emphasizes communications and interactions among stakeholders throughout the life of a project. Integrated process is a holistic decision making process based on systems thinking and life cycle approach.

interative process: A repetitive and circular process that helps a team to define goals and check ideas against these goals.

Integrated Pest Management (IPM): A sustainable approach to pest management.

LEED interpretations: Precedent-setting (project credit interpretation) rulings. A project team can opt into the LEED interpretation process when submitting an inquiry to GBCI.

leverage points: Places where a small interventions can generate big changes.

life cycle approach: Looking at a product or building through its entire life cycle.

life cycle assessment (LCA): Use life cycle thinking in environmental issues.

life cycle costing: Looking at the cost of purchasing and operating a building or product, and the relative savings.

low impact development (LID): A land development approach mimicking natural systems and managing storm water as close to the source as possible.

"Net-Zero": A project, which doesn't use any more resources than what it can produce. Similar concepts include carbon neutrality and water balance.

negative feedback loop: A signal for the system to stop changes when a response is not needed anymore.

open system: Resources are brought from the outside, consumed, and then disposed of as waste to the outside.

permaculture: Designing human habitats and agriculture systems based on models and relationships found in nature.

positive feedback loop: A stimulus causes an effect and encourages the loop to produce more of this effect.

Prius effect: Provides real time feedback of energy use so that users can adjust behaviors to save energy.

Project CIRs: LEED credit interpretation rulings for specific project circumstances.

retrocommissioning: A building tune-up that restores efficiency and improves performance.

regenerative: Regenerative buildings and communities evolve with living systems and help to renew resources and life. Regenerative projects generate electricity and sell the excess back to the grid, as well as return water to nature, which is cleaner than it was before use.

systems thinking: In a system, each component affects many other components. They are all related to each other.

Wingspread Principles on the US Response to Global Warming: A set of principles signed by organizations and individuals to express their commitment to address global warming. It calls for 60% to 80% reduction of greenhouse gas emission by midcentury (based on 1990 levels).

Back page promotion

You may be interested in some other books written by Gang Chen:

A. ARE Mock Exam series. See following link:
http://www.GreenExamEducation.com

B. LEED Exam Guides series. See following link:
http://www.GreenExamEducation.com

C. *Building Construction: Project Management, Construction Administration, Drawings, Specs, Detailing Tips, Schedules, Checklists, and Secrets Others Don't Tell You (Architectural Practice Simplified, 2nd edition)*
http://www.ArchiteG.com

D. *Planting Design Illustrated*
http://www.GreenExamEducation.com

ARE Mock Exam Series

Published ARE & California Supplemental Exam (CSE) books:
Project Planning & Design (PPD) ARE 5.0 Mock Exam (Architect Registration Examination): ARE 5.0 Overview, Exam Prep Tips, Hot Spots, Case Studies, Drag-and-Place, Solutions and Explanations
ISBN: 9781612650296

Project Development & Documentation (PDD) ARE 5.0 Mock Exam (Architect Registration Exam): ARE 5.0 Overview, Exam Prep Tips, Hot Spots, Case Studies, Drag-and-Place, Solutions and Explanations
ISBN: 9781612650258

Programming, Planning & Practice ARE Mock Exam (PPP of Architect Registration Exam): ARE Overview, Exam Prep Tips, Multiple-Choice Questions and Graphic Vignettes, Solutions and Explanations
ISBN-13: 9781612650067

Site Planning & Design ARE Mock Exam (SPD of Architect Registration Exam): ARE Overview, Exam Prep Tips, Multiple-Choice Questions and Graphic Vignettes, Solutions and Explanations
ISBN-13: 9781612650111

Building Design and Construction Systems (BDCS) ARE Mock Exam (Architect Registration Exam): ARE Overview, Exam Prep Tips, Multiple-Choice Questions and Graphic Vignettes, Solutions and Explanations
ISBN-13: 9781612650029

Schematic Design (SD) ARE Mock Exam (Architect Registration Exam): ARE Overview, Exam Prep Tips, Graphic Vignettes, Solutions and Explanations
ISBN-13: 9781612650050

Structural Systems ARE Mock Exam (SS of Architect Registration Exam): ARE Overview, Exam Prep Tips, Multiple-Choice Questions and Graphic Vignettes, Solutions and Explanations
ISBN-13: 9781612650012

Building Systems (BS) ARE Mock Exam (Architect Registration Exam): ARE Overview, Exam Prep Tips, Multiple-Choice Questions and Graphic Vignettes, Solutions and Explanations
ISBN-13: 9781612650036

Construction Documents and Service (CDS) Are Mock Exam (Architect Registration Exam): ARE Overview, Exam Prep Tips, Multiple-Choice Questions and Graphic Vignettes, Solutions and Explanations
ISBN-13: 9781612650005

Mock California Supplemental Exam (CSE of Architect Registration Exam): CSE Overview, Exam Prep Tips, General Section and Project Scenario Section, Questions, Solutions and Explanations
ISBN: 9781612650159

See the following link for the latest information on all our books:
http://www.**GreenExamEducation**.com

Check out FREE tips and info for all ARE Exams at **GeeForum**.com, you can post jpeg files of your vignettes or your questions for other users' review.

LEED Exam Guides Series: Comprehensive Study Materials, Sample Questions, Mock Exam, Building LEED Certification and Going Green

LEED (Leadership in Energy and Environmental Design) is the most important trend of development, and it is revolutionizing the construction industry. It has gained tremendous momentum and has a profound impact on our environment.

From LEED Exam Guides series, you will learn how to

1. Pass the LEED Green Associate Exam and various LEED AP + exams (each book will help you with a specific LEED exam).
2. Register and certify a building for LEED certification.
3. Understand the intent for each LEED prerequisite and credit.
4. Calculate points for a LEED credit.
5. Identify the responsible party for each prerequisite and credit.
6. Earn extra credit (exemplary performance) for LEED.
7. Implement the local codes and building standards for prerequisites and credit.
8. Receive points for categories not yet clearly defined by USGBC.

There is currently NO official GBCI book on the LEED Green Associate Exam, and most of the existing books on LEED and LEED AP are too expensive and too complicated to be practical and helpful. The LEED Exam Guides series fill in the blanks, demystify LEED, and uncover the tips, codes, and jargon for LEED as well as the true meaning of "going green." They will set up a solid foundation and fundamental framework of LEED for you. Each book in the LEED Exam Guides series covers every aspect of one or more specific LEED rating system(s) in plain and concise language and makes this information understandable to all people.

These books are small and easy to carry around. You can read them whenever you have a few extra minutes. They are indispensable books for all people—administrators; developers; contractors; architects; landscape architects; civil, mechanical, electrical, and plumbing engineers; interns; drafters; designers; and other design professionals.

Why is the LEED Exam Guides series needed?

A number of books are available that you can use to prepare for the LEED Exams:

1. *USGBC Reference Guides*. You need to select the correct version of the *Reference Guide* for your exam.

   The *USGBC Reference Guides* are comprehensive, and they give too much information. For example, *The LEED v4 Reference Guide for Green Building Design and Construction (BD&C)* has about 817 oversized pages. Many of the calculations in the books are too detailed for the exam. They are also expensive (approximately $200 each, so most people may not buy them for their personal use, but instead, will seek to share an office copy).

It is good to read a reference guide from cover to cover if you have the time. The problem is not too many people have time to read the whole reference guide. Even if you do read the whole guide, you may not remember the important issues to pass the LEED exam. You need to reread the material several times before you can remember much of it.

Reading the reference guide from cover to cover without a guidebook is a difficult and inefficient way of preparing for the LEED AP Exam, because you do NOT know what USGBC and GBCI are looking for in the exam.

2. The USGBC workshops and related handouts are concise, but they do not cover extra credits (exemplary performance). The workshops are expensive, costing approximately $450 each.

3. Various books published by a third party are available online. However, most of them are not very helpful.

There are many books on LEED, but not all are useful.

LEED Exam Guides series will fill in the blanks and become a valuable, reliable source:

a. They will give you more information for your money. Each of the books in the LEED Exam

Guides series has more information than the related USGBC workshops.

b. They are exam-oriented and more effective than the USGBC reference guides.

c. They are better than most, if not all, of the other third-party books. They give you comprehensive study materials, sample questions and answers, mock exams and answers, and critical information on building LEED certification and going green. Other third-party books only give you a fraction of the information.

d. They are comprehensive yet concise. They are small and easy to carry around. You can read them whenever you have a few extra minutes.

e. They are great timesavers. I have highlighted the important information that you need to understand and MEMORIZE. I also make some acronyms and short sentences to help you easily remember the credit names.

It should take you about 1 or 2 weeks of full-time study to pass each of the LEED exams. I have met people who have spent 40 hours to study and passed the exams.

You can find sample texts and other information about the LEED Exam Guide, and check out FREE tips on the easiest way to pass the LEED exams and info for all LEED Exams and ARE Exams at **GeeForum.com**, you can post your questions for other users' review.

What others are saying about *LEED Green Associate Exam Guide*...

"Finally! A comprehensive study tool for LEED Green Associate Prep!"
"I took the one-day Green LEED Green Associate course and walked away with a power point binder printed in very small print—which was missing MUCH of the required information (although I didn't know it at the time). I studied my little heart out and took the test, only to fail it by 1 point. Turns out I did NOT study all the material I needed to in order to pass the test. I found this book, read it, marked it up, retook the test, and passed it with a 95%. Look, we all know the LEED Green Associate Exam is new and the resources for study are VERY limited. This one's the VERY best out there right now. I highly recommend it."
—Consultant VA

"Complete overview for the LEED Green Associate exam"
"I studied this book for about three days and passed the exam ... if you are truly interested in learning about the LEED system and green building design, this is a great place to start."
—K.A. Evans

"Very effective study guide"
"I purchased both this study guide and Mr. Chen's LEED GA Mock Exams book and found them to be excellent tools for preparing for the LEED Green Associate Exam. While Mr. Chen's LEED Green Associate Exam Guide is not perfect (in that it's not the most user-friendly presentation of the material), it was very effective in at least presenting most, if not all, of the topics that the exam touched upon. While I wouldn't necessarily recommend

my abbreviated strategy for preparing for the exam, the following worked for me: I read through the exam guide a couple of times (but not word for word), took the mock exam and referenced the guide for explanations for any wrong answers, did the same for the two mock exams in Mr. Chen's LEED GA Mock Exams book, flipped through the documents that Mr. Chen recommends, and took two other web-based mock exams that I purchased on eBay. Literally after ten hours of preparation time, I took the actual exam and passed with a 189, thanks in large part to Mr. Chen's books. If I decide to take one of the LEED AP exams in the future, I will definitely be picking up more of Mr. Chen's study materials."
—shwee "shwee"

"Only study guide needed to pass on your first try"
"I don't write reviews, but I'm compelled to for this purchase. This was the only book I read and studied to prepare for the LEED Green Associate exam, and passed with ease on the first try today. I was over prepared for the exam by using this study guide, which is what I wanted on exam day. I bought the book, read it three times, learned a lot of good information, saved valuable time, and passed on the first try. By the way, I'm not a good test taker. I don't agree with any of the negative reviews that are posted... I'm glad I ignored those when I made the purchase and went with the majority. THIS PRODUCT DELIVERED THE RESULTS, CASE CLOSED. I'll be buying his *LEED AP BD&C Exam Guide* to prepare for the specialty exam. Thank you Mr. Gang Chen!!!"
—Lobo

"I just finished taking the LEED Green Associate Exam and, thankfully, I passed it on the first try by using this book as my primary study guide...I particularly liked the way the author organized the information within it."
—**Lewis Colon**

Note: Other books in the **LEED Exam Guides series** *are in the process of being produced. At least* **One book will eventually be produced for each of the LEED exams.** *The series include:*

LEED v4 Green Associate Exam Guide (LEED GA): *Comprehensive Study Materials, Sample Questions, Mock Exam, Green Building LEED Certification, and Sustainability*, LEED Exam Guide series, ArchiteG.com. Latest Edition.

LEED GA MOCK EXAMS (LEED v4): *Questions, Answers, and Explanations: A Must-Have for the LEED Green Associate Exam, Green Building LEED Certification, and Sustainability*, LEED Exam Guide series, ArchiteG.com. Latest Edition

LEED v4 BD&C EXAM GUIDE: *A Must-Have for the LEED AP BD+C Exam: Comprehensive Study Materials, Sample Questions, Mock Exam, Green Building Design and Construction, LEED Certification, and Sustainability*, LEED Exam Guide series, ArchiteG.com. Latest Edition.

LEED v4 BD&C MOCK EXAMS: *Questions, Answers, and Explanations: A Must-Have for the LEED AP BD+C Exam, Green Building LEED Certification, and Sustainability*, LEED Exam Guide series, ArchiteG.com. Latest Edition.

LEED AP Exam Guide: *Study Materials, Sample Questions, Mock Exam, Building LEED Certification, and Going Green,* LEED Exam Guides series, LEEDSeries.com. Latest Edition.

LEED ID&C EXAM GUIDE: *A Must-Have for the LEED AP ID+C Exam: Comprehensive Study Materials, Sample Questions, Mock Exam, Green Interior Design and Construction, LEED Certification, and Sustainability*, LEED Exam Guide series, ArchiteG.com. Latest Edition.

LEED O&M EXAM GUIDE: *A Must-Have for the LEED AP O+M Exam: Comprehensive Study Materials, Sample Questions, Mock Exam, Green Building Operations and Maintenance, LEED Certification, and Sustainability*, LEED Exam Guide series, ArchiteG.com. Latest Edition.

LEED HOMES EXAM GUIDE: *A Must-Have for the LEED AP Homes Exam: Comprehensive Study Materials, Sample Questions, Mock Exam, Green Building LEED Certification, and Sustainability*, LEED Exam Guide series, ArchiteG.com. Latest Edition.

LEED ND EXAM GUIDE: *A Must-Have for the LEED AP Neighborhood Development Exam: Comprehensive Study Materials, Sample Questions, Mock Exam, Green Building LEED Certification, and Sustainability*, LEED Exam Guide series, ArchiteG.com. Latest Edition.

How to order these books:
You can order the books listed above at:
http://www.GreenExamEducation.com

Check out FREE tips and info for all LEED Exams at **GeeForum**.com, you can post your questions for other users' review.

Building Construction

Project Management, Construction Administration, Drawings, Specs, Detailing Tips, Schedules, Checklists, and Secrets Others Don't Tell You (Architectural Practice Simplified, 2nd edition)

Learn the Tips, Become One of Those Who Know Building Construction and Architectural Practice, and Thrive!

For architectural practice and building design and construction industry, there are two kinds of people: those who know, and those who don't. The tips of building design and construction and project management have been undercover—until now.

Most of the existing books on building construction and architectural practice are too expensive, too complicated, and too long to be practical and helpful. This book simplifies the process to make it easier to understand and uncovers the tips of building design and construction and project management. It sets up a solid foundation and fundamental framework for this field. It covers every aspect of building construction and architectural practice in plain and concise language and introduces it to all people. Through practical case studies, it demonstrates the efficient and proper ways to handle various issues and problems in architectural practice and building design and construction industry.

It is for ordinary people and aspiring young architects as well as seasoned professionals in the construction industry. For ordinary people, it uncovers the tips of building construction; for aspiring architects, it works as a construction industry survival guide and a guidebook to shorten the process in mastering architectural practice and climbing up the professional ladder; for seasoned architects, it has many checklists to refresh their memory. It is an indispensable reference book for ordinary people, architectural students, interns, drafters, designers, seasoned architects, engineers, construction administrators, superintendents, construction managers, contractors, and developers.

You will learn:
1. How to develop your business and work with your client.
2. The entire process of building design and construction, including programming, entitlement, schematic design, design development, construction documents, bidding, and construction administration.
3. How to coordinate with governing agencies, including a county's health department and a city's planning, building, fire, public works departments, etc.
4. How to coordinate with your consultants, including soils, civil, structural, electrical, mechanical, plumbing engineers, landscape architects, etc.
5. How to create and use your own checklists to do quality control of your construction documents.
6. How to use various logs (i.e., RFI log, submittal log, field visit log, etc.) and lists (contact list, document control list, distribution list, etc.) to organize and simplify your work.
7. How to respond to RFI, issue CCDs, review change orders, submittals, etc.
8. How to make your architectural practice a profitable and successful business.

Planting Design Illustrated
A Must-Have for Landscape Architecture: A Holistic Garden Design Guide with Architectural and Horticultural Insight, and Ideas from Famous Gardens in Major Civilizations

One of the most significant books on landscaping!

This is one of the most comprehensive books on planting design. It fills in the blanks of the field and introduces poetry, painting, and symbolism into planting design. It covers in detail the two major systems of planting design: formal planting design and naturalistic planting design. It has numerous line drawings and photos to illustrate the planting design concepts and principles. Through in-depth discussions of historical precedents and practical case studies, it uncovers the fundamental design principles and concepts, as well as the underpinning philosophy for planting design. It is an indispensable reference book for landscape architecture students, designers, architects, urban planners, and ordinary garden lovers.

What Others Are Saying About *Planting Design Illustrated* **...**

"I found this book to be absolutely fascinating. You will need to concentrate while reading it, but the effort will be well worth your time."
—**Bobbie Schwartz, former president of APLD (Association of Professional Landscape Designers) and author of** *The Design Puzzle: Putting the Pieces Together.*

"This is a book that you have to read, and it is more than well worth your time. Gang Chen takes you well beyond what you will learn in other books about basic principles like color, texture, and mass."
—**Jane Berger, editor & publisher of gardendesignonline**

"As a longtime consumer of gardening books, I am impressed with Gang Chen's inclusion of new information on planting design theory for Chinese and Japanese gardens. Many gardening books discuss the beauty of Japanese gardens, and a few discuss the unique charms of Chinese gardens, but this one explains how Japanese and Chinese history, as well as geography and artistic traditions, bear on the development of each country's style. The material on traditional Western garden planting is thorough and inspiring, too. *Planting Design Illustrated* definitely rewards repeated reading and study. Any garden designer will read it with profit."
—**Jan Whitner, editor of the *Washington Park Arboretum Bulletin***

"Enhanced with an annotated bibliography and informative appendices, *Planting Design Illustrated* offers an especially "reader friendly" and practical guide that makes it a very strongly recommended addition to personal, professional, academic, and community library gardening & landscaping reference collection and supplemental reading list."
—**Midwest Book Review**

"Where to start? *Planting Design Illustrated* is, above all, fascinating and refreshing! Not something the lay reader encounters every day, the book presents an unlikely topic in an easily digestible, easy-to-follow way. It is superbly

organized with a comprehensive table of contents, bibliography, and appendices. The writing, though expertly informative, maintains its accessibility throughout and is a joy to read. The detailed and beautiful illustrations expanding on the concepts presented were my favorite portion. One of the finest books I've encountered in this contest in the past 5 years."
—Writer's Digest 16th Annual International Self-Published Book Awards Judge's Commentary

"The work in my view has incredible application to planting design generally and a system approach to what is a very difficult subject to teach, at least in my experience. Also featured is a very beautiful philosophy of garden design principles bordering poetry. It's my strong conviction that this work needs to see the light of day by being published for the use of professionals, students & garden enthusiasts."
—Donald C. Brinkerhoff, FASLA, chairman and CEO of Lifescapes International, Inc.

Index

40/60 rule, 38, 93
Albedo, 33, 45, 71, 101, 121
American Council for an Energy Efficient Economy (ACEEE), 91, 92
ammonia (NH3), 50
APPA, 68, 117
association factors, 149
BAS, 75, 83, 125
Basic Services, 98
blackwater, 31, 51, 102, 105
Blackwater, 87
Bleed-off, 70, 120, 123
CFC, 30, 35, 36, 45, 49, 50, 86, 91, 100, 102, 104
CIBSE, 84, 137
CIR, 43, 50, 51, 98, 105, 158
CPESC, 85, 139
Cradle-to-cradle, 45, 100
Daylighting, 71, 83, 122, 136
Diverted materials, 116
ECTC, 140
Energy Policy Act (EPAct), 31, 32, 88

ENERGY STAR products, 74, 124
ENERGY STAR rating, 124, 135, 139
EPP, 75, 126
FAR, 30, 41, 87, 96
FSC-certified wood, 68, 117
FTE, 165
GBCI, 15, 147
graywater, 31, 36, 44, 51, 87, 91, 100, 105
green power, 33, 52, 101
Green Seal, 75, 88, 126, 144
Green-e, 33, 35, 45, 63, 66, 89, 91, 114
GWP, 43, 49, 50, 98, 102, 103, 104, 105
Halon, 36, 92
Heat Island, 52, 106
I-BEAM, 70, 81, 120, 133
Impact Categories, 149
IPM, 85, 140, 177
LEED, 181, 185, 186, 187, 188, 191, 192
LEED AP, 14, 147
LEED Rating System Selection Policy, 93, 173

LEED v4, 150, 156
LEED-NC, 7
Legionella pneumophila, 73, 78, 123, 130
Level 1 walk-through analysis, 63, 141
Level II Energy Audit, 86
Life cycle analysis, 45
Light pollution, 70, 71, 121
Mnemonics, 94
Naturally Ventilated Spaces, 131, 137
NERC, 89, 145
Note, 191
ODP, 37, 43, 47, 48, 50, 98, 102, 103, 104
Open spaces, 90
photopollution, 121
PPD, 182
process energy, 29, 85
RECs, 45, 71, 75, 101, 126

Recycled content, 116
Recycled materials, 30, 87, 116
Regional Priority, 32, 88
regulated (non-process) energy, 29, 86
ROI, 39, 95
Seal of Approval program, 66, 114
Setpoints, 75, 125
SR, 107
SRI, 33, 37, 43, 45, 52, 71, 87, 89, 98, 101, 107, 121, 142
stormwater, 30, 37, 43, 87, 92, 98
Tips, 181, 183, 194
vegetated roof, 30, 52, 106, 107
weighting process, 150
Zero Emission Vehicles (ZEV), 35, 91

www.ingramcontent.com/pod-product-compliance
Lightning Source LLC
Chambersburg PA
CBHW052119300426
44116CB00010B/1728